The recognition of patterns is a creative way to have students develop understanding for the concept of multiplication. Pattern analysis should be part of the elementary study in mathematics as it is also viewed as foundational skills for algebraic reasoning.

Michael Kestner
Mathematics and Science Partnership Program
Office of Elementary and Secondary Education/United States Department of Education

Teach Your Child the Multiplication Tables is everything I think a multiplication workbook should be, and my daughter thinks it's lots of fun. Set around a circus theme, the book is child-friendly with lots of pictures, large print, and plenty of space for writing the answers. The best part of this book, however, is that rote memorization is not the goal, rather understanding the inherent patterns is.

My daughter works through this workbook at her own pace, whenever she's in the mood for it, and she's already had quite a few "ah-ha!" moments as she recognizes and predicts the various patterns.

Ruth Pell
California Homeschool News

Many children struggle learning and recalling multiplication facts, and need other techniques rather than rote memorization to master these skills. Eugenia Francis' workbook utilizes wonderful, brain-compatible strategies and methods to do so – such as learning to recognize and attend to patterns for each of the multiplication tables, using memory tricks/mnemonics, and other engaging and fun techniques. I recommend **Teach Your Child the Multiplication Tables** as a helpful resource for children to learn the math facts and understand the principles of multiplication.

Sandra Rief, author of **How to Reach & Teach Children with ADD/ADHD**
co-author of **How to Reach & Teach All Children in the Inclusive Classroom**

Teach Your Child the Multiplication Tables is a wonderfully entertaining, clear, and memorable way to understand multiplication and to learn the times tables! Younger students will also benefit from this book; cute characters and cartoon creatures appear on each page. As soon as the book arrived, my 5 year old daughter was eager to work on it. **Teach Your Child the Multiplication Tables** is one of my top picks for 3rd graders at www.mathmom.com

Linda Burks
Los Altos, California

An ONLINE INTERVIEW with HOME EDUCATION MAGAZINE can be found at: www.homeedmag.com/blogs/resources/?p=206. In the interview, Eugenia Francis discusses the benefits of her method for children with special needs.

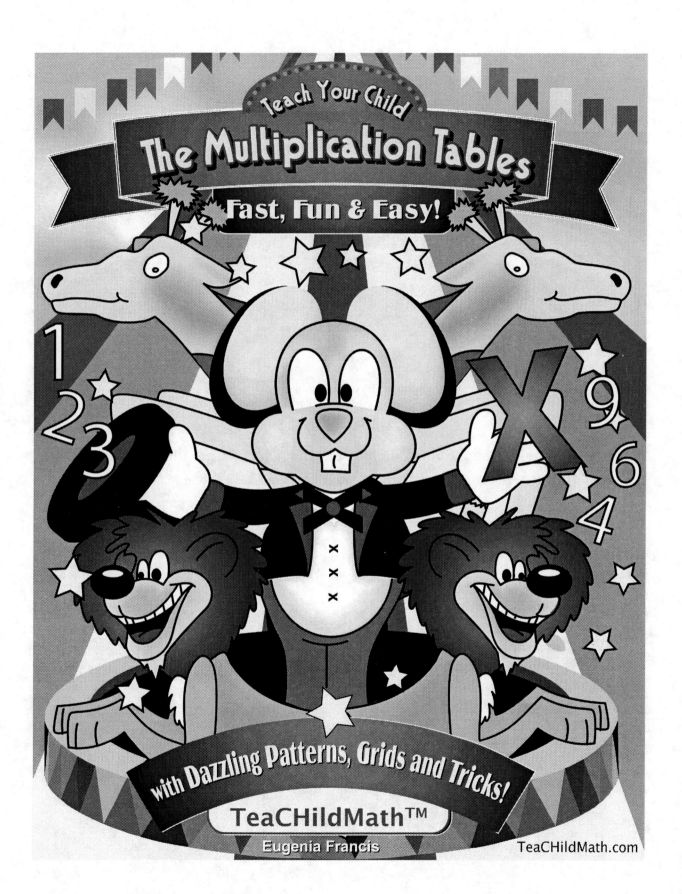

ISBN 0-7414-2081-3

Special thanks to illustrators Michael Likens & Rudy Rodriguez at Gopixel and of course my son, Scott Francis, who inspired this journey.

Published by:

PUBLISHING.COM

1094 New Dehaven Street, Suite 100
West Conshohocken, PA 19428-2713
Info@buybooksontheweb.com
www.buybooksontheweb.com
Toll-free (877) BUY BOOK
Local Phone (610) 941-9999
Fax (610) 941-9959

∞

Printed in the United States of America

Printed on Recycled Paper

Published April 2006

Table of Contents

Included in the above are review sheets to
reinforce learning & evaluate progress.

Introduction

Like most third graders, my son Scott found learning the multiplication tables a challenge. After an afternoon of tiresome drills, I decided there had to be an easier way than rote memorization.

At the kitchen table, I drew a grid: numbers 1-10 horizontally and 1-10 vertically. Pencil in hand, Scott filled in the 1's, the 2's, the 5's and the 10's. I immediately saw these were the tables with a nice, easy pattern. Well, then, I asked myself, what were the nice, easy patterns for the rest of the tables? I remembered a pattern for the 9's. Using the grid, I had Scott pencil in 0-9 down the 9 column and then 9-0 to the right of these numbers. "There, you know the 9's!" I said. Scott was amazed by this trick. The 9's, he decided, were super easy!

If the 9's had a trick, were there not other tricks or patterns? We rapidly discovered an even number multiplied by an even number was always even. The 2, 4, 6 and 8 tables had to end in some combination of 2-4-6-8-0 which we found repeated mid-grid after 10, 20, 30 and 40 in the 2, 4, 6 and 8 tables respectively. Pretty cool, Scott thought.

What other patterns could we see such as whether the multiple would be odd or even? Odd multiples we discovered were few in number. Why? Because an EVEN number times ANY number (ODD or EVEN) is even. An odd multiple results ONLY when an ODD number multiplies another ODD. Thus, we arrived at one of the Great Truths of multiplication:

Even x Even = EVEN

Even x Odd = EVEN

Odd x Even = EVEN

<u>Odd x Odd = ODD</u>

Each time Scott filled in a grid for a new table, I had him fill in other tables he had learned.   Rather than learning each table in isolation, he learned each in context of the others. With new tables, he could predict whether the multiple would be odd or even. Each pattern or "trick" boosted his confidence. Scott learned by doing.

Like many children, Scott was a visual learner. My method based on "dazzling patterns, grids and tricks," helped him discern patterns, integrate the concept of multiplication and actually made multiplication fun. Designed for Grades 2 and 3, this workbook is also suitable for children with special learning needs. Your child will learn the multiplication tables and develop critical thinking skills.

Teach Your Child the Multiplication Tables, Fast, Fun and Easy, with Dazzling Patterns, Grids and Tricks will instill in your child a love of numbers and confidence in math.

Included in each lesson are review sheets to evaluate progress. Detach the exercises in this workbook so your child will not be tempted to glance at following pages for the answer.

Discovery makes learning fun!

Crazy, Crazy Circus!

It's a wild night at the Magic Circus!
The circus train roared into the Big Top.
Monkeys climbed out. Lions jumped out.
Giraffes leaped out. Elephants broke out.
Bears hopped out. Clowns tumbled out.
Monkeys, lions, giraffes, elephants, bears and
clowns are everywhere!
Balloons and balls are everywhere!
The Magic Circus is a Crazy, Crazy Circus!
Ringmaster Rudy needs your help!
How many monkeys, giraffes, elephants, bears
and clowns are there in the Magic Circus?
It will take too long to count!
It will take too long to add!
Monkeys, giraffes, elephants, bears and clowns
have to do their acts!
Let's help Rudy find patterns and multiply!
Here's your ticket to the Magic Circus!

ADMIT
ONE

Find a Pattern and Multiply

You can COUNT objects one by one but this is so *s-l-o-w.*
You can find a pattern and ADD but this is too *s-l-o-w.*
Or you can find a pattern, MULTIPY and go *fast!*

Count	**Add**	**Multiply**
	4	4 x 6 = 24
	4	4 six times = 24
	4	
	4	
	4	4
	+4	x6
24	24	24
24 steps	**6 steps**	**1 step!**
So slow	Slow	*Fast!*

Look for patterns, each appeared in groups of **4.**

There were 6 rows of   .

You can **ADD:** 4+4+4+4+4+4=24 **SLOW**

You can **MULTIPLY:** 4 X 6 = 24 *FAST!!!!*

Name _____

Look for PATTERNS

2 six times is the same as **6 two times**

Turn page sideways to check

6 x 2 = 12
2 x 6 = 12

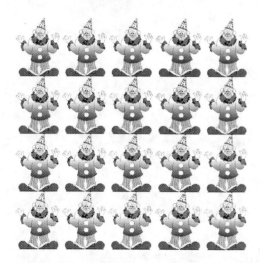

Fill in: 5 x 4 = 20

Find the pattern

5 four times?

Turn the page sideways

4 five times?

5 x 4 = 20

Fill in: 9 x 2 = 18

Find the pattern
9 two times?
2 nine times?

2 x 9 = 18

Find a pattern and multiply:

$$\underline{5} \times \underline{3} = \underline{15}$$
$$\underline{3} \times \underline{5} = \underline{15}$$

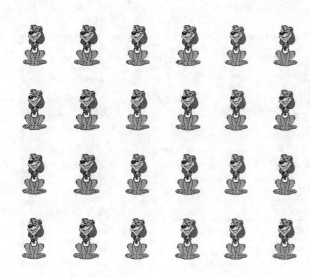

$$\underline{6} \times \underline{4} = \underline{24}$$
$$\underline{4} \times \underline{6} = \underline{24}$$

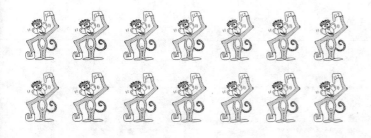

$$\underline{7} \times \underline{2} = \underline{14}$$
$$\underline{2} \times \underline{7} = \underline{14}$$

$$\underline{5} \times \underline{1} = \underline{5}$$
$$\underline{1} \times \underline{5} = \underline{5}$$

How Do Numbers Multiply?

Let's Multiply the Dots and See

Multiply 3 x 2 on the grid.
What do you discover when you turn the page sideways?
**Three dots two times is the same as two dots
three times.   3 x 2 = 6   2 x 3 = 6**
Now multiply 2 x 3.

X	1	2	3	4	5
1	•	••	•••	••••	•••••
2	⋮	∷	(••• •••)	•••• ••••	••••• •••••
3	⋮	(∷ ∷)	••• ••• •••	•••• •••• ••••	••••• ••••• •••••
4	⋮	∷ ∷	••• ••• ••• •••	•••• •••• •••• ••••	••••• ••••• ••••• •••••
5	⋮	∷ ∷	••• ••• ••• ••• •••	•••• •••• •••• •••• ••••	••••• ••••• ••••• ••••• •••••

Table 2 Magic

Name _____

2-4-6-8-0!

After 10, repeat the **2-4-6-8-0** pattern.
Multiply 2 x table across.
Super easy, isn't it?

X	1	2	3	4	5	6	7	8	9	10
1		2								
2		4								
3		6								
4		8								
5		10								
6		1_								
7		1_								
8		1_								
9		1_								
10		2_								

Fill in the
darkened squares.

X	1	2	3	4	5	6	7	8	9	10
1										
2										
3										
4										
5										
6										
7										
8										
9										
10										

Fill in the
darkened squares.

X	1	2	3	4	5	6	7	8	9	10
1										
2										
3										
4										
5										
6										
7										
8										
9										
10										

Ringmaster Rudy's Review

Let's help Rudy fill in the blanks

2 x <u>5</u> = 10	3 x 2 = 6	9 x 0 = 0
8 x 2 = 16	4 x 10 = 40	8 x ___ = 64
2 x 6 = 12	5 x 2 = 10	1 x 10 = 10
4 x 2 = 8	2 x 9 = 18	6 x 10 = 60
2 x 3 = 6	7 x 2 = 14	2 x 8 = 16
5 x 0 = 0	3 x 1 = 3	9 x 2 = 18
2 x 7 = 14	7 x 10 = 70	2 x 10 = 20
5 x 10 = 50	4 x 1 = 4	2 x 4 = 8
9 x 10 = 90	6 x 2 = 12	3 x 10 = 30

If You Know the 2 x Table,
You Know the 8's!

Fill in the 8 x table. Notice the last digits repeat the **2-4-6-8**
pattern of the 2 x table in *reverse* order.
0 always follows the last number in the pattern.
The **8-6-4-2-0** pattern repeats after 40.
Fill in 2 and 8 across

X	1	2	3	4	5	6	7	8	9	10
1		2						8		
2		4						16		
3		6						24		
4		8						32		
5		10						40		
6		12						4_		
7		14						5_		
8		16						6_		
9		18						7_		
10		20						8_		

Table 8 Review

Fill in the missing numbers for the 8 x table.
Do you notice a pattern?
What fill-in number appears twice? _____
Super easy! Fill in 2 and 8 across.

X	1	2	3	4	5	6	7	8	9	10
1		2						8		
2		4						_6		
3		6						_4		
4		8						_2		
5		10						_0		
6		12						_8		
7		14						_6		
8		16						_4		
9		18						_2		
10		20						_0		

Let's help Ringmaster Rudy
with the Magic Circus.

How many giraffes in total? ___ x ___ = ___

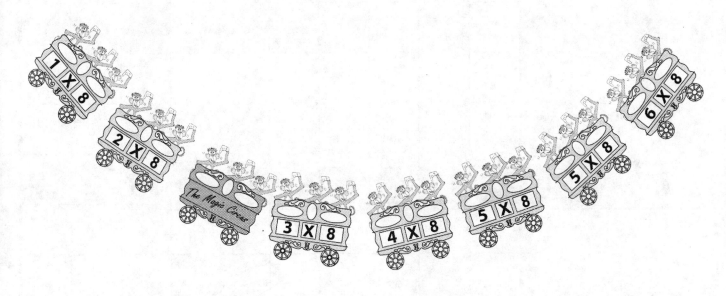

How many monkeys in total? ___ x ___ = ___

Name _____

Fill in the columns for 2 & 8.
Notice the multiples of the 8 x table
are 4 times larger than the 2's.
Example: 2 & 8, 10 & 40.
Why is that?

X	1	2	3	4	5	6	7	8	9	10
1										
2	2	4	6	8	10	12	14	16	18	20
3										
4										
5										
6										
7										
8	8	16	24	32	40	48	56	64	72	80
9										
10										

Name _____

4-8-2-6-0

Now you know the 4 x table!

Fill in 4 x table. Notice the **4-8-2-6-0** pattern repeats after 20. Pretty cool, isn't it? Fill in 4 across.

X	1	2	3	4	5	6	7	8	9	10
1				4						
2				8						
3				12						
4				16						
5				20						
6				2_						
7				2_						
8				3_						
9				3_						
10				4_						

Fill in the
darkened squares.

X	1	2	3	4	5	6	7	8	9	10
1										
2										
3										
4										
5										
6										
7										
8										
9										
10										

Table 4 Review

Fill in 4 x table.
Test your skills with
tables 2 and 8.

	2	4	8
1	2	4	8
2	_	8	1_
3	_	_2	2_
4	_	_6	3_
5	10	20	40
6	1_	2_	4_
7	1_	2_	5_
8	1_	3_	6_
9	1_	3_	7_
10	20	40	80

Name _____

Grid Magic

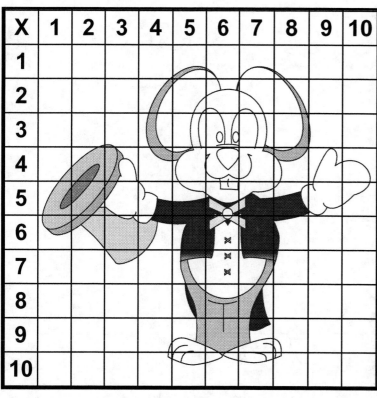

Can you copy Rudy on the blank grid?

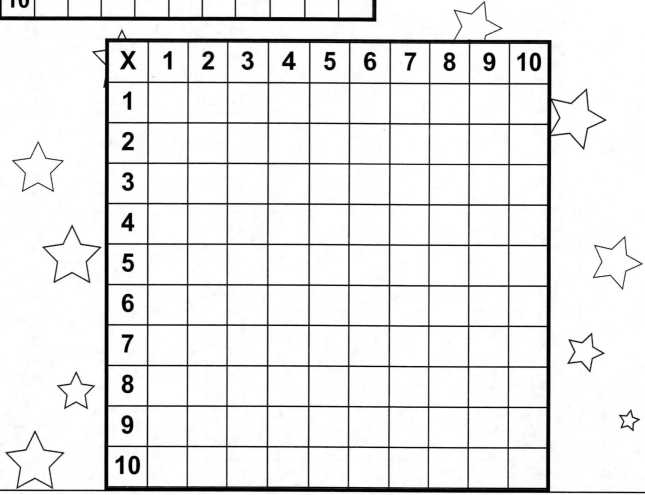

20   TeaCHildMath™

Circus Snacks

Hot Dogs $3
Pretzels $1
Cotton Candy $2

Ice Cream $2
Popcorn $3
Soda $1

Erica bought 8 pretzels
at the circus for her friends.
How much did she spend?

_____ x _____ = $_____

Tom bought his 4 brothers
each a soda.
How much did he spend?

_____ x _____ = $_____

The twins bought 4 bags of
popcorn and 4 sodas.
How much did they spend?

_____ x _____ = $_____
_____ x _____ = $_____

Total:

_____ + _____ = $_____

Martha bought 8 ice cream
bars and 10 sodas.
How much did she spend?

_____ x _____ = $_____
_____ x _____ = $_____

Total:

_____ + _____ = $_____

Carlos and Billy bought 4 hot
dogs, 3 sodas and 2 ice creams.
How much did they spend?

_____ x _____ = $_____
_____ x _____ = $_____
_____ x _____ = $_____

Total:

_____ + ___ + ___ = $_____

Lucy bought her family 6 sodas,
5 pretzels and 8 hot dogs.
How much did she spend?

_____ x _____ = $_____
_____ x _____ = $_____
_____ x _____ = $_____

Total:

_____ + ___ + ___ = $_____

2 and 4 Magic!

Fill in the columns for 2 & 4. Notice the multiples of the
4 x table are 2 times larger than the 2's. Why is that?

X	1	2	3	4	5	6	7	8	9	10
1										
2	2	4	6	8	10	12	14	16	18	20
3										
4	4	8	12	16	20	24	28	32	36	40
5										
6										
7										
8										
9										
10										

Name _____

Fill in the columns for 4 & 8. Notice the multiples of the 8 x table are 2 times larger than the 4's. Why is that?

X	1	2	3	4	5	6	7	8	9	10
1										
2										
3										
4	4	8	12	16	20	24	28	32	36	40
5										
6										
7										
8	8	16	24	32	40	48	56	64	72	80
9										
10										

Name _____

2 and 4 Magic Review
Fill in the darkened squares.

X	1	2	3	4	5	6	7	8	9	10
1										
2										
3										
4										
5										
6										
7										
8										
9										
10										

4 and 8 Magic Review
Fill in the darkened squares.

X	1	2	3	4	5	6	7	8	9	10
1				■				■		
2				■				■		
3				■				■		
4	■	■	■	■	■	■	■	■	■	■
5				■				■		
6				■				■		
7				■				■		
8	■	■	■	■	■	■	■	■	■	■
9				■				■		
10				■				■		

Name _____

Fill in the columns for 2, 4 and 8.

X	2		4		8
1	2		4		8
2	_		_		1_
3	_		1_		2_
4	_		1_		3_
5	10		20		40
6	1_		2_		4_
7	1_		2_		5_
8	1_		3_		6_
9	1_		3_		7_
10	20		40		80

Magic Circus Fun

Help Rudy solve the following:

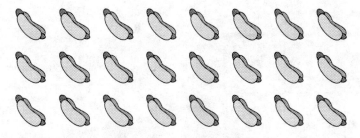

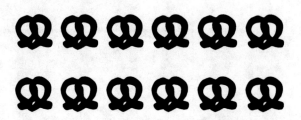

_8_ x _3_ = __

__ x __ = __

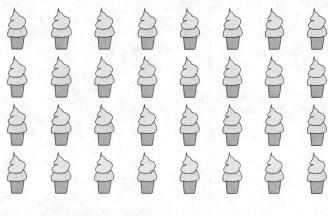

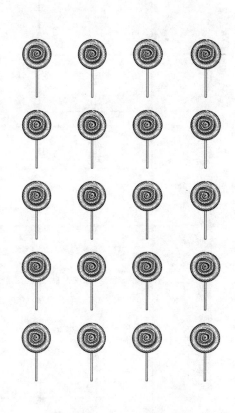

__ x __ = __

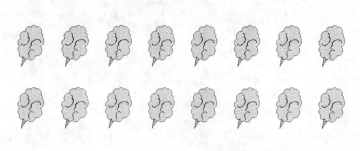

__ x __ = __

__ x __ = __

2, 4 & 8 Mastery!

Fill in the columns for
2, 4 and 8.

X		2		4		8
1		2		4		8
2		—		—		—
3		—		—		—
4		—		—		—
5		10		20		40
6		—		—		—
7		—		—		—
8		—		—		—
9		—		—		—
10		20		40		80

Name _____

Test your skill with 2, 4 and 8 tables. Can you fill in 6?
It too has a pattern.

X	2	4	6	8
1	2	4	<u>6</u>	8
2	_	_	1<u>2</u>	1_
3	_	1_	1<u>8</u>	2_
4	_	1_	2<u>4</u>	3_
5	10	20	3<u>0</u>	40
6	1_	2_	3_	4_
7	1_	2_	4_	5_
8	1_	3_	4_	6_
9	1_	3_	5_	7_
10	20	40	60	80

Wouldn't you know? It's 6-2-8-4-0

Fill in the 6 x table. Notice the 6-2-8-4-0 pattern repeats after 30. Fill in 6 across.

 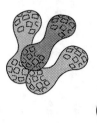  

X	1	2	3	4	5	6	7	8	9	10
1						6				
2						12				
3						18				
4						24				
5						30				
6						3_				
7						4_				
8						4_				
9						5_				
10						6_				

PEANUTS
ELEPHANT
BRAND

2, 4, 6 and 8 Magic!

Fill in the columns for 2, 4, 6 & 8.

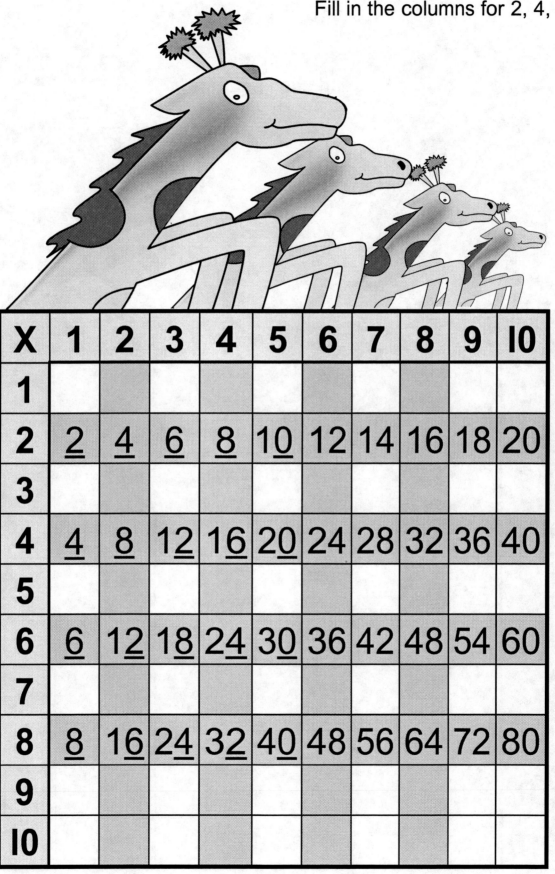

X	1	2	3	4	5	6	7	8	9	10
1										
2	2	4	6	8	10	12	14	16	18	20
3										
4	4	8	12	16	20	24	28	32	36	40
5										
6	6	12	18	24	30	36	42	48	54	60
7										
8	8	16	24	32	40	48	56	64	72	80
9										
10										

2,4,6 and 8 Magic Review

Fill in the
darkened squares.

X	1	2	3	4	5	6	7	8	9	10
1										
2										
3										
4										
5										
6										
7										
8										
9										
10										

Crisscross 2 & 8, 4 & 6

The pattern for table 8 is the **reverse** of table 2, followed by a 0.
The pattern for table 6 is the **reverse** of table 4, followed by a 0.
Can you fill in the rest?

X	2		8		4		6
1	2		8		4		6
2	4		_6		8		_2
3	6		_4		_2		_8
4	8		_2		_6		_4
5	_0		_0		_0		_0
6	_2		_8		_4		_6
7	_4		_6		_8		_2
8	_6		_4		_2		_8
9	_8		_2		_6		_4
10	_0		_0		_0		_0

Name _____

Remember the patterns?

2 x table : 2-4-6-8 followed by a **0**.
8 x table : 8-6-4-2 followed by a **0**.
4 x table : 4-8-2-6 followed by a **0**.
6 x table : 6-2-8-4 followed by a **0**.

Can you fill in the rest?

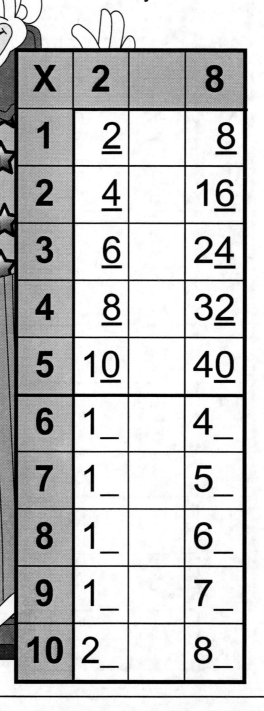

X	2		8
1	2		8
2	4		16
3	6		24
4	8		32
5	10		40
6	1_		4_
7	1_		5_
8	1_		6_
9	1_		7_
10	2_		8_

4		6
4		6
8		12
12		18
16		24
20		30
2_		3_
2_		4_
3_		4_
3_		5_
4_		6_

Magic Circus Fun

Help Rudy solve the following:

There are ____ elephants in the ring. Each elephant has ____ balloons. How many balloons are there?

____ x ____ = ____

There are ____ clowns in the ring. Each clown has ____ balls. How many balls are there?

____ x ____ = ____

There are ____ monkeys in the ring. Each monkey has ____ lollipops. How many lollipops are there?

____ x ____ = ____

Crisscross Challenge!

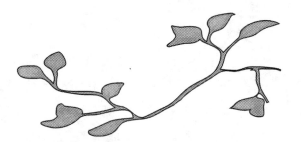

Fill in tables 2, 8, 4 and 6.

X	2		8
1	2		8
2	–		–
3	–		–
4	–		–
5	10		40
6	–		–
7	–		–
8	–		–
9	–		–
10	20		80

4		6
4		6
–		–
–		–
–		–
20		30
–		–
–		–
–		–
–		–
40		60

Name _____

Help Rudy solve the following:

__ x __ = __

__ x __ = __

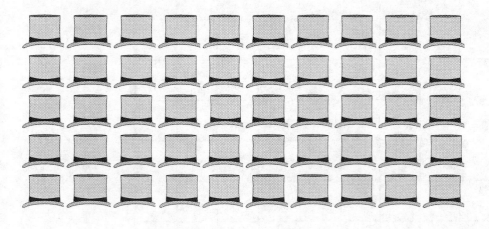

__ x __ = __

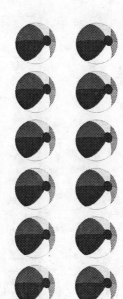

__ x __ = __

Grid Magic

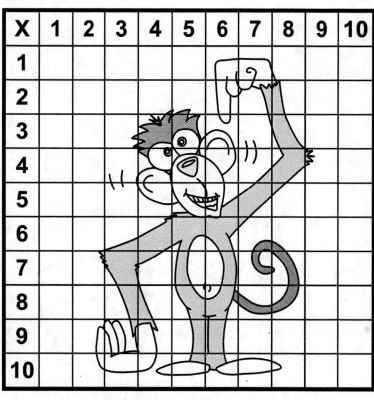

X	1	2	3	4	5	6	7	8	9	10
1										
2										
3										
4										
5										
6										
7										
8										
9										
10										

Can you copy Sam on the blank grid?

X	1	2	3	4	5	6	7	8	9	10
1										
2										
3										
4										
5										
6										
7										
8										
9										
10										

Rudy's Secret Code for 2, 4, 6 & 8!

1st clue: the pattern repeats after 10, 20, 30, and 40.
2nd secret clue: 8 x table pattern is 2 x table in **reverse**.
3rd secret clue: 6 x table pattern is 4 x table in **reverse**.
4th secret clue: tables 2, 4, 6 & 8 end in some combination
of **2-4-6-8** followed by a **0**.

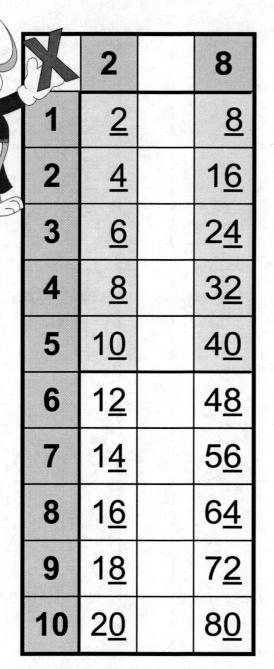

X	2		8
1	2		8
2	4		16
3	6		24
4	8		32
5	10		40
6	12		48
7	14		56
8	16		64
9	18		72
10	20		80

4	6
4	6
8	12
12	18
16	24
20	30
24	36
28	42
32	48
36	54
40	60

Remember the Secret Code?

Secret Clue: patterns repeat after 10, 20, 30 & 40.

X	2		8
1	2		8
2	4		16
3	6		24
4	8		32
5	10		40
6	1_		4_
7	1_		5_
8	1_		6_
9	1_		7_
10	2_		8_

4		6
4		6
8		12
12		18
16		24
20		30
2_		3_
2_		4_
3_		4_
3_		5_
4_		6_

Name _____

Color the Clown

Solve the problems to color the clown. Choose your own colors for the face and hat.

Color Key

6 - yellow
12 - red
16 - green
20 - blue
24 - orange
36 - purple

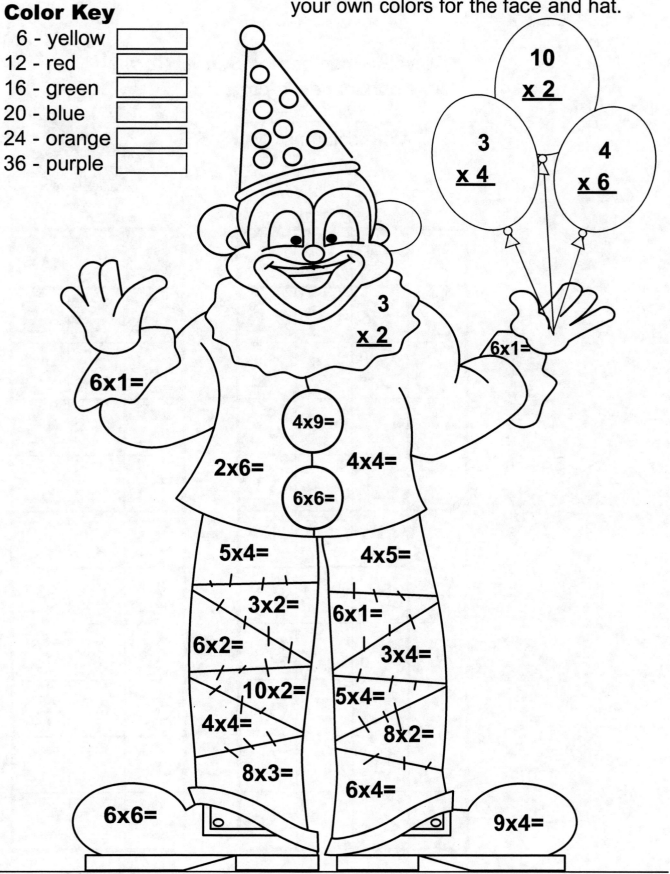

10
x 2

3
x 4

4
x 6

3
x 2

6x1=

6x1=

4x9=

2x6=

4x4=

6x6=

5x4=

4x5=

3x2=

6x1=

6x2=

3x4=

10x2=

5x4=

4x4=

8x2=

8x3=

6x4=

6x6=

9x4=

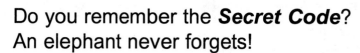

Do you remember the **Secret Code**?
An elephant never forgets!

Fill in the columns.

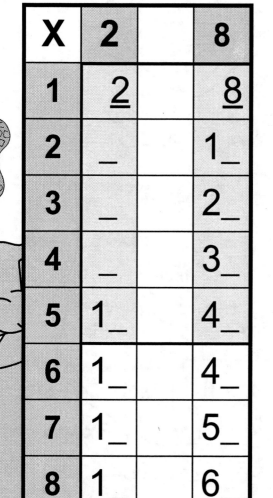

X	2		8
1	2		8
2	_		1_
3	_		2_
4	_		3_
5	1_		4_
6	1_		4_
7	1_		5_
8	1_		6_
9	1_		7_
10	2_		8_

4		6
4		6
_		1_
1_		1_
1_		2_
2_		3_
2_		3_
2_		4_
3_		4_
3_		5_
4_		6_

Let's help Rudy solve the following:

8 x 3 = 24   4 x 6 = 24   8 x 7 = 56

2 x 7 = 14   4 x 9 = 36   9 x 6 = 54

4 x 4 = ~~16~~   5 x 6 = 30   6 x 7 = 42

2 x 8 = 16   8 x 4 = 32   9 x 8 = 72

0 x 8 = 0   8 x 9 = 72   6 x 8 = 48

2 x 3 = 6   4 x 10 = 40   8 x 8 = 64

8 x 5 = 37   6 x 4 = 24   8 x 6 = 48

4 x 3 = 12   3 x 6 = 18   6 x 3 = 18

2 x 7 = 12   4 x 8 = 32   8 x 7 = 56

5 x 2 = 10   5 x 4 = 20   6 x 6 = 36

2 x 7 = 12   8 x 2 = 16   3 x 6 = 18

2 x 10 = 20   8 x 3 = 24   3 x 10 = 30

6 x 6 = 36   4 x 10 = 40   10 x 10 = 100

Secret Code Challenge!

Fill in the columns.

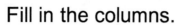

X	2		8
1	2		8
2	–		–
3	–		–
4	–		–
5	10		40
6	–		–
7	–		–
8	–		–
9	–		–
10	20		80

4		6
4		6
–		–
–		–
–		–
20		30
–		–
–		–
–		–
–		–
40		60

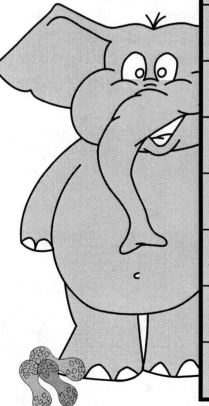

Circle all the even multiples.
What did you discover?

EVEN number x **EVEN** number = _____
EVEN number x **ODD** number = _____

X	1	2	3	4	5	6	7	8	9	10
1	1	2	3	4	5	6	7	8	9	10
2	2	4	6	8	10	12	14	16	18	20
3	3	6	9	12	15	18	21	24	27	30
4	4	8	12	16	20	24	28	32	36	40
5	5	10	15	20	25	30	35	40	45	50
6	6	12	18	24	30	36	42	48	54	60
7	7	14	21	28	35	42	49	56	63	70
8	8	16	24	32	40	48	56	64	72	80
9	9	18	27	36	45	54	63	72	81	90
10	10	20	30	40	50	60	70	80	90	100

Decoding Patterns?
Write the multiplication problem for:

2 rows of 10 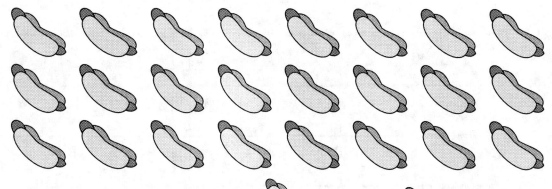s = ____ s

2 x 10 = ____

___ **rows of** ___ s = ____ s

___ **x** ___ = ____

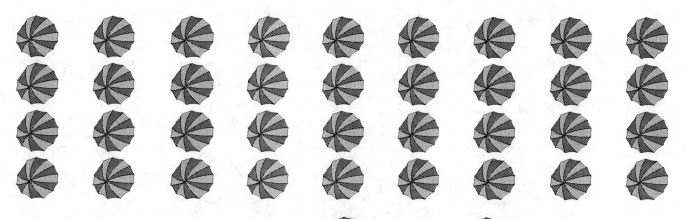

___ **rows of** ___ s = ____ s

___ **x** ___ = ____

Name _____

Multiplying Evens

Fill in the white squares for
tables 2, 4, 6, 8 and 10.

X	1	2	3	4	5	6	7	8	9	10
1										
2										
3										
4										
5										
6										
7										
8										
9										
10										

Clown Derby

Race to the Finish

Fill in the blanks.

3 x ___ = 24   8 x ___ = 56   6 x ___ = 42

4 x ___ = 12   5 x ___ = 30   7 x ___ = 28

1 x ___ = 10   9 x ___ = 72   2 x ___ = 10

6 x ___ = 18   4 x ___ = 16   3 x ___ = 30

2 x ___ = 16   8 x ___ = 40   5 x ___ = 10

7 x ___ = 14   9 x ___ = 36   6 x ___ = 54

5 x ___ = 40   3 x ___ = 12   4 x ___ = 20

8 x ___ = 72   8 x ___ = 32   6 x ___ = 48

4 x ___ = 24   8 x ___ = 48   3 x ___ = 18

5 x ___ = 50   2 x ___ = 18   2 x ___ = 20

6 x ___ = 24   8 x ___ = 64   6 x ___ = 36

4 x ___ = 36   **Good Job!**   2 x ___ = 14

Odd or Even?

Even X Even = **EVEN**

Even X Odd = **EVEN**   Odd X Even = **EVEN**

Odd X Odd = **ODD**

Notice the **hopscotch pattern** of the **odd** multiples.
Turn the page sideways. Notice 4 x 2 is the **same**
as 2 x 4. Check out the other dot multiples.

X	1	2	3	4	5
1	•	••	•••	••••	•••••
2	:	::	:::	::::	:::::
3	⋮	::	:::	::::	:::::
4	⋮	::	:::	::::	:::::
5	⋮	::	:::	::::	:::::

Can You Multiply the DOTS?

Even X Even = **EVEN**

Even X Odd = **EVEN**   Odd X Even = **EVEN**

Odd X Odd = **ODD**

Fill in with the correct dot multiple. Notice the
DARK squares represent ODD multiples.

X	1	2	3	4	5
1	•	••	•••	••••	•••••
2					
3					
4					
5					

Magic Circus Fun

Help Rex complete the pattern
and find his way home to
99 Magic Circus Drive.

1 3 5 7 9 11 21 41 31 51 71 61 Rex 81 99 91

Odd or Even?

Circle each pair of :

[bicycle illustrations arranged in 4 rows of 8]

Do the same with [two images] :

With [two images] :

[rows of pinwheel illustrations]

8 [bike]s 4 times = <u>32</u> [bike]s

8 X 4 = 32

When you grouped in pairs, were any [bike]s left over?

Yes ____ No __✓__

32 is an <u>even</u> number.

5 [image]s 5 times = ____ [image]s

5 X 5 = 25

When you grouped in 2's, were any [image]s left over?

Yes ____ No ____

25 is an _____ number.

9 [image]s 3 times = ____ [image]s

9 X 3 = ___

Were any [image]s left over?

Yes ____ No____

Odd ____ or Even ____

1, 3, 5, 7, 9 or any number ending in 1, 3, 5, 7, 9 are **ODD**.
2, 4, 6, 8, 0 or any number ending in 2, 4, 6, 8, 0 are **EVEN**.

Circle each pair of  :

Any ⭐ s left over.

$7 \times 1 = 7$

7 is an _____ number.

Any ⭐ s left over.

$7 \times 2 = 14$

14 is an _____ number.

Any ⭐ s left over.

$7 \times 3 = 21$

21 is an _____ number.

Secret Clues to Multiplication:
Odd number X **Odd** = ODD
Odd number x **Even** = EVEN
Even number x **Even** = EVEN
Even Number x **ANY** number = EVEN

Odd x Odd = ODD
All other multiples are Even:
Odd x Even = EVEN
Even X Odd = EVEN
Even x Even = EVEN

Odd or Even?

Instead of multiples, fill in with **odd** or **even**.
Secret Clue: if one number is **even**, the multiple is **even**. Circle every **even** number first.

6 x 3 = <u>even</u>	3 x 7 = <u>odd</u>	8 x 2 = <u>even</u>
7 x 7 = ____	9 x 8 = ____	5 x 3 = ____
9 x 3 = ____	8 x 8 = ____	4 x 7 = ____
7 x 9 = ____	2 x 9 = ____	5 x 8 = ____
5 x 6 = ____	9 x 9 = ____	6 x 4 = ____
7 x 5 = ____	2 x 6 = ____	9 x 1 = ____
6 x 7 = ____	5 x 5 = ____	3 x 3 = ____
3 x 2 = ____	9 x 4 = ____	6 x 9 = ____
4 x 1 = ____	7 x 8 = ____	8 x 3 = ____
10 x 7 = ____	1 x 8 = ____	4 x 3 = ____
6 x 8 = ____	2 x 7 = ____	9 x 5 = ____
2 x 2 = ____	4 x 5 = ____	7 x 1 = ____

Multiplying Odds and Evens

Fill in each square with an **e** for **Even** or an **o** for **Odd**.
Notice the **hopscotch** pattern for **ODD** numbers.
Amazing fact:
Even x Even = Even
Even x Odd = Even
Odd x Odd = Odd

X	1	2	3	4	5	6	7	8	9	10
1	o	e								
2	e	e								
3										
4										
5										
6										
7										
8										
9										
10										

Table 5 Hopscotch 5-0-5-0!

Fill in the 5 column. **Clue:** last digits have a **5 - 0 pattern.**
Remember: **5** x an **EVEN** number ends in **0.**
5 x an **ODD** number ends in **5.**
Fill in across. Check your answers with the 5 column.

X	1	2	3	4	5	6	7	8	9	10
1					5					
2					1_					
3					15					
4					2_					
5					25					
6					3_					
7					35					
8					4_					
9					45					
10					5_					

Name ____________________________

Magic Circus Fun

Help Sam complete the pattern
and find his way home to
150 Magic Circus Drive.

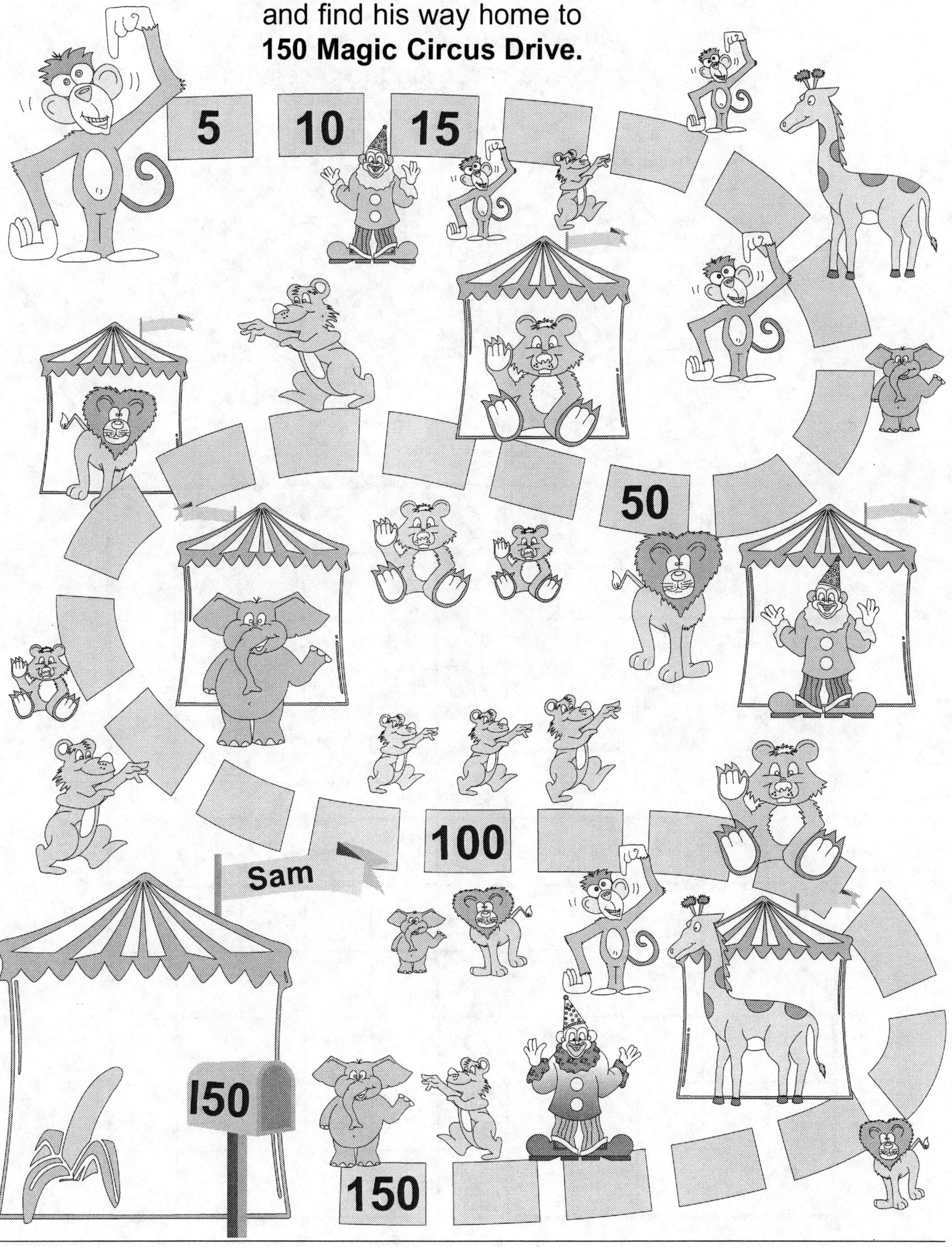
5
10
15
50
100
Sam
150
150

Name _____

Hop on 10, 20, 30, 40, 50! Oh, so nifty!

Fill in the blanks and then across for 5 x table.
Check your answers with the 5 column.

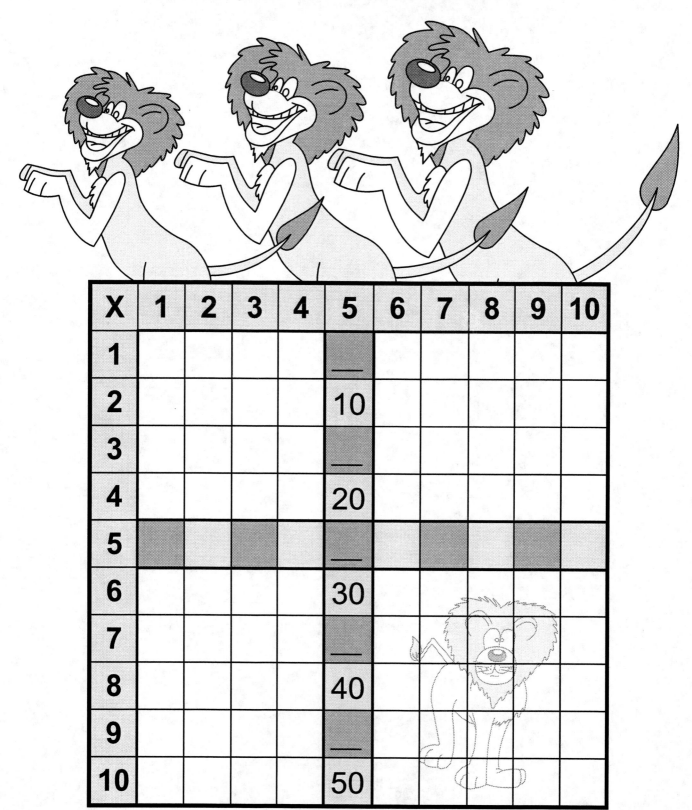

X	1	2	3	4	5	6	7	8	9	10
1					—					
2					10					
3					—					
4					20					
5					—					
6					30					
7					—					
8					40					
9					—					
10					50					

5 and 10 Magic!
Fill in tables 5 and 10.
How much larger are the multiples of the 10 x table?
Example: 5 & 10, 30 & 60. Why is that?

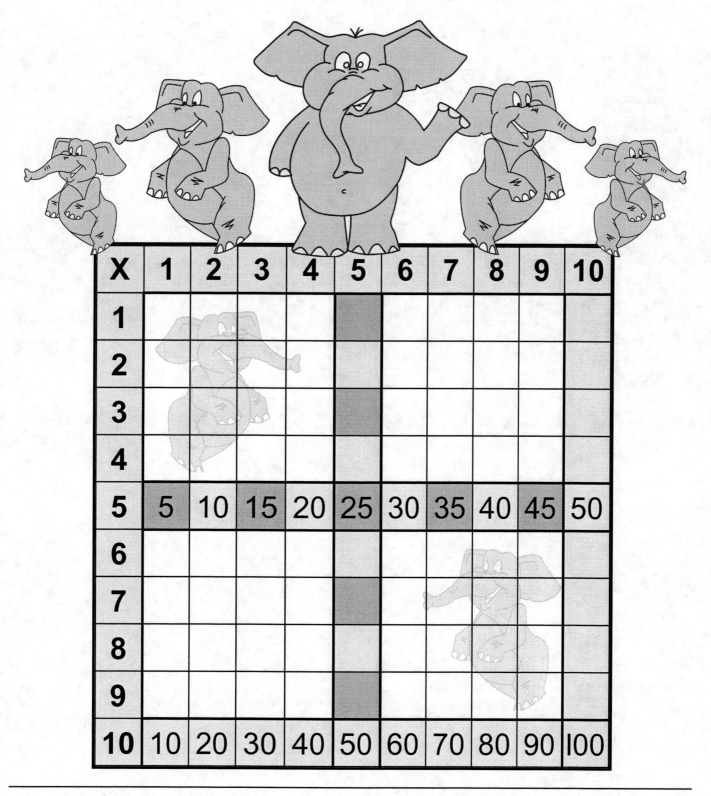

X	1	2	3	4	5	6	7	8	9	10
1										
2										
3										
4										
5	5	10	15	20	25	30	35	40	45	50
6										
7										
8										
9										
10	10	20	30	40	50	60	70	80	90	100

5 and 10 Magic Review

Fill in tables 5 and 10.

X	1	2	3	4	5	6	7	8	9	10
1										
2										
3										
4										
5										
6										
7										
8										
9										
10										

Name _____

Circus Fun

Help Rudy multiply the following.
Underneath, write the Odd/Even rule.

5 x 5 = _____   10 x 3 = _____   7 x ___ = 35

<u>O</u> x <u>O</u> = ODD   ___ x ___ = _____   ___ x ___ = _____

6 x ___ = 30   2 x ___ = 20   8 x 5 = _____

___ x ___ = _____   ___ x ___ = _____   ___ x ___ = _____

3 x 5 = _____   10 x 10 = _____   2 x ___ = 10

___ x ___ = _____   ___ x ___ = _____   ___ x ___ = _____

4 x 5 = _____   5 x ___ = 50   9 x ___ = 45

___ x ___ = _____   ___ x ___ = _____   ___ x ___ = _____

___ x ___ = 30   ___ x ___ = 25   ___ x ___ = 10

___ x ___ = _____   ___ x ___ = _____   ___ x ___ = _____

Multiply:

5	5	5	5	8	4	7	3	10
<u>x2</u>	<u>x5</u>	<u>x6</u>	<u>x9</u>	<u>x5</u>	<u>x5</u>	<u>x5</u>	<u>x5</u>	<u>x5</u>

1, 5 and 10 Challenge!

Fill in tables 1, 5 and 10.

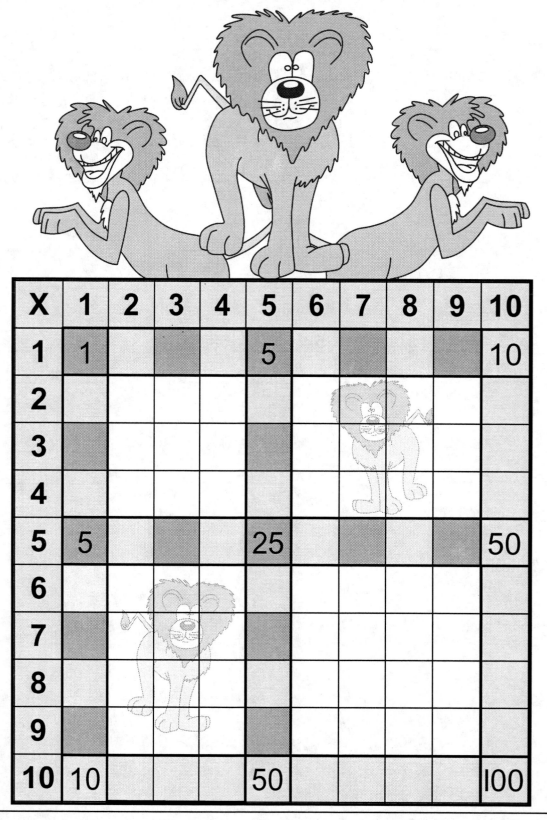

X	1	2	3	4	5	6	7	8	9	10
1	1				5					10
2										
3										
4										
5	5				25					50
6										
7										
8										
9										
10	10				50					100

Name _____

Circus Snack Survey

Children voted for their favorite Circus Snacks. Here are the results:

★ = 10 votes

1. Which snack got 50 votes? _____

2. How many votes did ice cream get? _____

3. Which snack got more votes than peanuts? _____

4. Which snack was the least favorite? _____

5. Which snack got 100 votes? _____

6. Which was the most popular snack? _____

7. Which of the above is your favorite snack?

_____

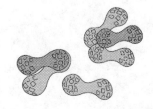  

The Trick to the 9's!

Part 1

Number **9** to **0** on the right.

X	9
1	_
2	1_
3	2_
4	3_
5	4_
6	5_
7	6_
8	7_
9	8_
10	9_

Circus Tickets

Adults $5   Children $2

Anna bought 6 children's tickets. How much did she spend?

$2 x 6 = $12

Mrs. Robles bought 5 adult tickets. How much did she spend?

____ x ____ = $____

Coach bought 9 children's tickets and 6 adult tickets. How much did he spend?

$2 x 9 = $18

$5 x 6 = $30

$18
+$30
Total: $48

Joe's aunt bought the family 3 adult tickets and 7 children's tickets.
How much did she spend?

____ x ____ = $____
____ x ____ = $____

Add the numbers.
Total: $____

Maria had a party at the circus. Her mother bought 4 adult tickets and 5 children's tickets. How much did they spend?

____ x ____ = $____
____ x ____ = $____

Add the numbers.
Total: $____

Betty spent $21 on circus tickets. She spent $15 on adult tickets How many adults were in her group? How many children were in the group?

$5 x ____ = $15
Adults: ____

$2 x ____ = $6
Children: ____

$21
-$15
Total: $6

Trick to the 9's

Part 2

Number **0** to **9** on the left.

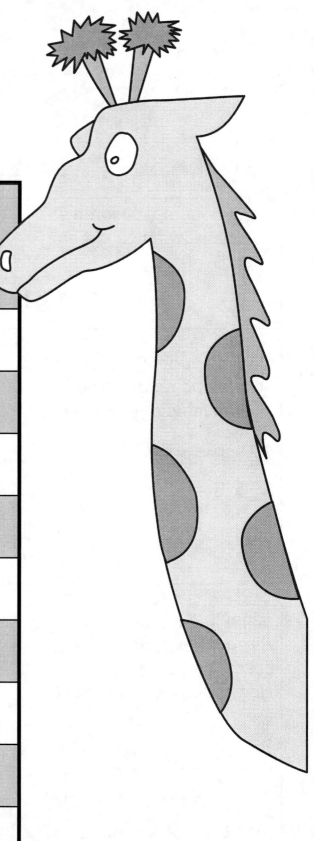

X	9
1	_0_9
2	_8
3	_7
4	_6
5	_5
6	_4
7	_3
8	_2
9	_1
10	_9_0

Decoding Patterns

Write the multiplication problem for:

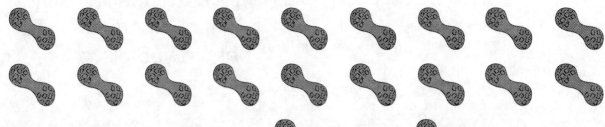

2 rows of 9 🥜 **s = ____** 🥜 **s**

2 x 9 = ____

even x odd = ____

___ **rows of** ___ 🐘 **s =** ____ 🐘 **s**

___ **x** ___ **=** ____

odd x ____ **=** ____

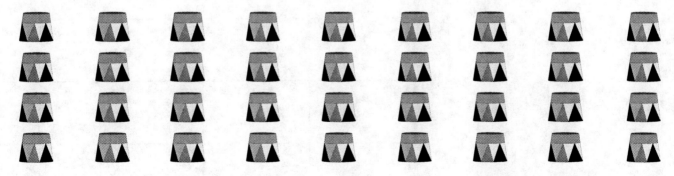

___ **rows of** ___ 🥁 **s =** ____ 🥁 **s**

___ **x** ___ **=** ____

___ **x** ___ **=** ____

Name _____

Magic 9's!
Separate the multiples into individual numbers and ADD.
What did you discover?

X	9	Add	Total
1	9	0+9=	9
2	18	1+8=	
3	27		
4	36		
5	45		
6	54		
7	63		
8	72		
9	81		
10	90		

Name _____

Magic Circus Fun

Help Rudy multiply the following.
Underneath, write the Odd/Even rule.

9 x 4 = ____   3 x 9 = ____   8 x ___ = 72
___ x ___ = Even   ___ x ___ = ____   ___ x ___ = ____

2 x ___ = 18   7 x ___ = 63   5 x ___ = 45
___ x ___ = ____   ___ x ___ = ____   ___ x ___ = ____

9 x 7 = ____   9 x 10 = ____   9 x ___ = 54
___ x ___ = ____   ___ x ___ = ____   ___ x ___ = ____

9 x ___ = 27   9 x ___ = 81   9 x ___ = 36
___ x ___ = ____   ___ x ___ = ____   ___ x ___ = ____

Multiply:

9	9	9	9	8	4	2	6	10
x7	x3	x5	x9	x9	x9	x9	x9	x9

The 9's *Flip Flop!*

Flip flop the multiples.
What did you discover?

X	9		
1	09		90
2	18		81
3	27		
4	36		
5	45		
6	54		
7	63		
8	72		
9	81		
10	90		

Grid Magic

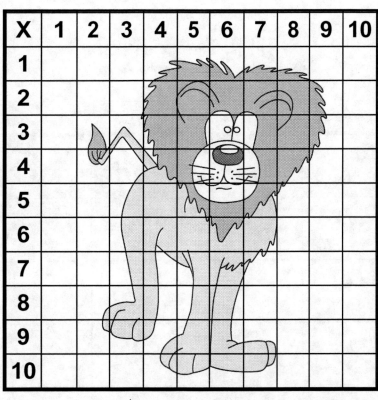

Can you copy Leo on the blank grid?

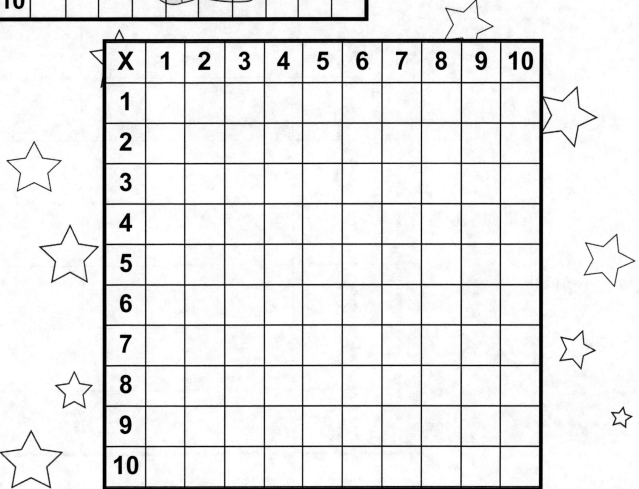

Name _____

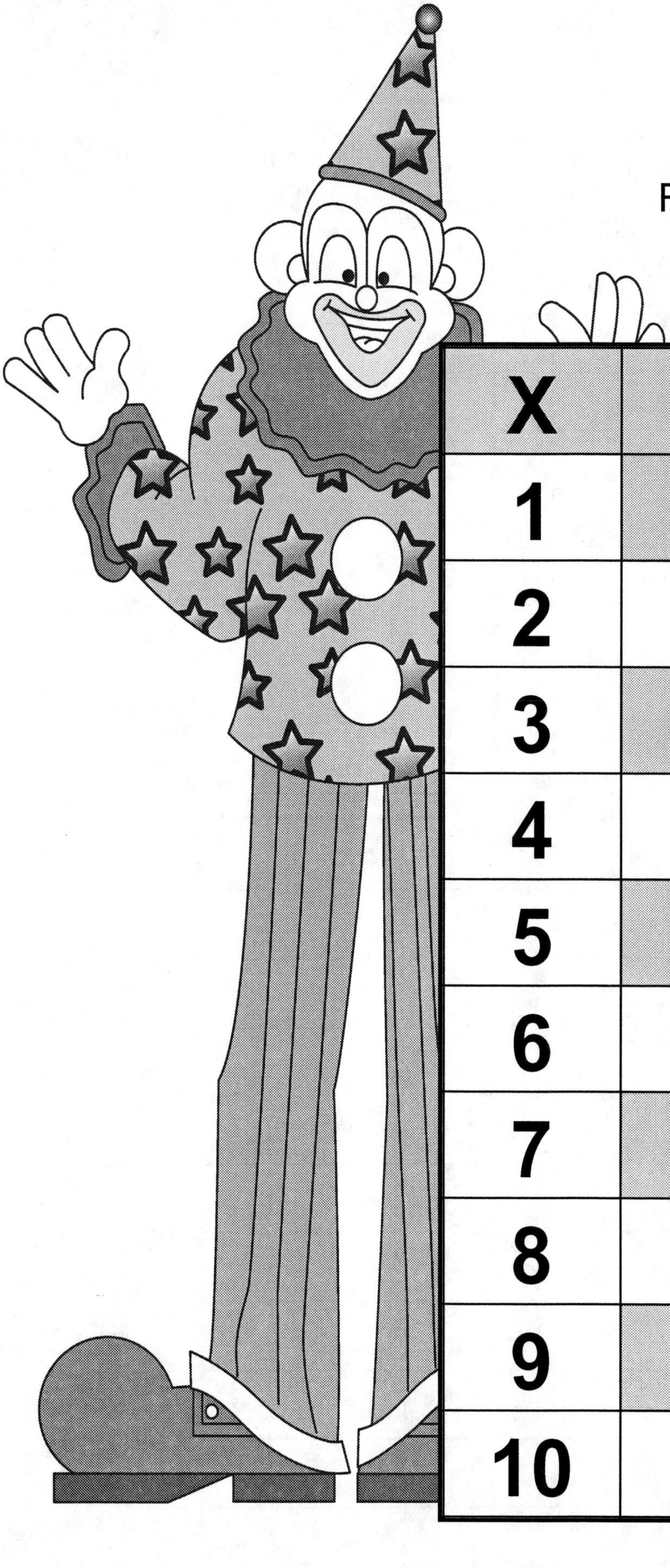

Fill in the columns.

X	9	Add	Total
1			
2			
3			
4			
5			
6			
7			
8			
9			
10			

_____

Name _____

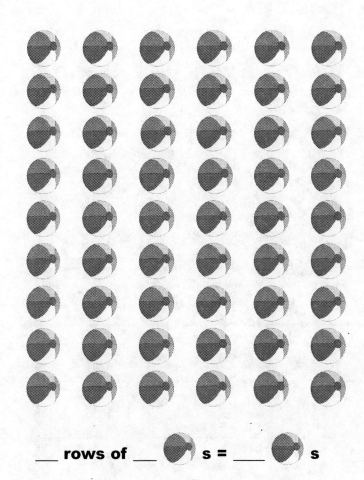

___ rows of ___ 🏐 s = ___ 🏐 s

___ x ___ = ___

___ rows of ___ 🍦 s = ___ 🍦 s

___ x ___ = ___

___ rows of ___ 🥨 s = ___ 🥨 s

___ x ___ = ___

Table 9 Hopscotch

Notice the hopscotch pattern between Odd and Even.
Odd X Odd = Odd. Odd x Even = Even. Fill in 9 across.

X	1	2	3	4	5	6	7	8	9	10
1									9	
2									18	
3									27	
4									36	
5									45	
6									54	
7									63	
8									72	
9									81	
10									90	

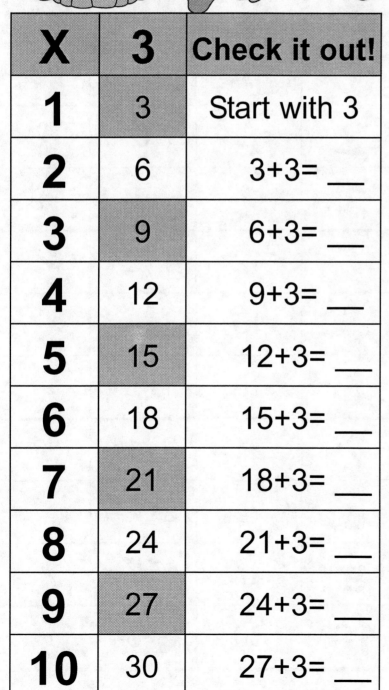

Mastering the 3's

The 3 times table is super easy!
Fill in the _____ by adding 3 to the
previous number.

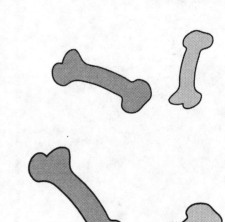

X	3	Check it out!
1	3	Start with 3
2	6	3+3= __
3	9	6+3= __
4	12	9+3= __
5	15	12+3= __
6	18	15+3= __
7	21	18+3= __
8	24	21+3= __
9	27	24+3= __
10	30	27+3= __

Trick to the 3's!
3-6-9, we're doing fine!
Can you discover the trick to the 3's?

X	3	Add	Total
1	3	3	3
2	6	6	6
3	9	9	9
4	12	1+2=	
5	15	1+5=	
6	18	1+8=	
7	21	2+1=	
8	24	2+4=	
9	27	2+7=	
10	30	3+0=	

Name _____

Help Rudy solve the following:

There are _____ giraffes in each ring.
How many giraffes in total?

_____ x _____ = _____

There are _____ monkeys in each ring.
How many monkeys in total?

_____ x _____ = _____

There are _____ lions in each ring.
How many lions in total?

_____ x _____ = _____

The 3's Once More!

Fill in the rest.

X	3	Add	Total
1	3	3	3
2	6	6	6
3	9	9	9
4	12	1+2=	3
5			
6			
7			
8			
9			
10			

Name _____

Help Leo complete the pattern
and find his way home to
102 Magic Circus Drive.

Magic Circus Fun

3 6 9

30

60

Leo

102

90

Name _____

Cool Trick to the 6's!

Although 6 is an **EVEN** number, it is a **multiple of 3**.
It too must have a trick. Can you discover it?
(For 6 x 8, there are 2 steps.)

X	6	Add	Total
1	6	0+6=	6
2	12	1+2=	
3	18	1+8=	
4	24	2+4=	
5	30	3+0=	
6	36	3+6=	
7	42	4+2=	
8	48	4+8=12 1+2=	
9	54	5+4=	
10	60	6+0=	

Circus Snack Survey

Children voted for their favorite Circus Snacks.
Here are the results:

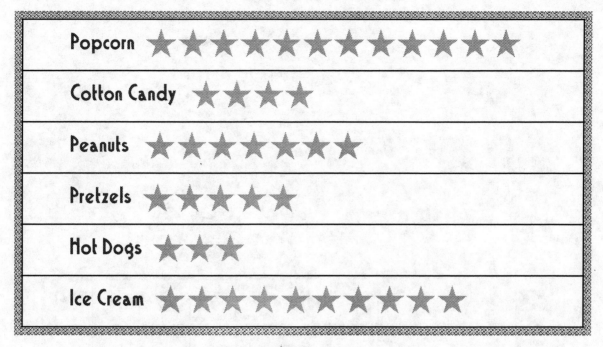

= 6 votes

1. Which snack got 60 votes? _____

2. How many votes did hot dogs get? _____

3. Which snacks got more votes than peanuts? _____

4. Which snack got 42 votes? _____

5. Which was the most popular snack? _____

6. Which snack was the least favorite? _____

Name _____

3 and 6 Magic!

Fill in tables 3 and 6. How much larger are the multiples of the 6 x table?
Example: 3 & 6, 30 & 60. Why is that?

X	1	2	3	4	5	6	7	8	9	10
1										
2										
3	3	6	9	12	15	18	21	24	27	30
4										
5										
6	6	12	18	24	30	36	42	48	54	60
7										
8										
9										
10										

Tricks of the 3, 6, 9 Tables
3-6-9   6-3-9   9-9-9

A super easy chart to help you remember!

X	3	Add	6	Add	9	Add
1	3	0+3=3	6	0+6=6	9	0+9=9
2	6	0+6=6	12	1+2=3	18	1+8=9
3	9	0+9=9	18	1+8=9	27	2+7=9
4	12	1+2=3	24	2+4=6	36	3+6=9
5	15	1+5=6	30	3+0=3	45	4+5=9
6	18	1+8=9	36	3+6=9	54	5+4=9
7	21	2+1=3	42	4+2=6	63	6+3=9
8	24	2+4=6	48	4+8=12 1+2=3	72	7+2=9
9	27	2+7=9	54	5+4=9	81	8+1=9
10	30	3+0=3	60	6+0=6	90	9+0=9

3, 6 and 9 Magic!

Fill in tables 3, 6 and 9.
Notice the hopscotch pattern of ODD multiples.

X	1	2	3	4	5	6	7	8	9	10
1										
2										
3	3	6	9	12	15	18	21	24	27	30
4										
5										
6	6	12	18	24	30	36	42	48	54	60
7										
8										
9	9	18	27	36	45	54	63	72	81	90
10										

Name _____

Circus Snacks

Hot Dogs $3
Pretzels $1
Cotton Candy $2

Ice Cream $2
Popcorn $3
Soda $1

Jim bought 6 bags of popcorn at the
circus for his friends.
How much did he spend?

_____ X _____ = $_____

Maria bought her sisters 5 pretzels.
How much did she spend?

_____ X _____ = $_____

Sue's sister bought 2 cotton candies and
3 sodas.
How much did she spend?

_____ X _____ = $_____

_____ X _____ = $_____

Total:
_____ + _____ = $_____

Coach bought the team 9 hot dogs and 10
sodas.
How much did he spend?

_____ X _____ = $_____

_____ X _____ = $_____

Total:
_____ + _____ = $_____

Bill and Tom were hungry. They bought 6
hot dogs, 4 sodas and 3 ice creams.
How much did they spend?

_____ X _____ = $_____

_____ X _____ = $_____

_____ X _____ = $_____

Total:
_____ +_____ + _____ = $_____

Alicia bought her family 5 sodas, 6 pretzels
and 7 hot dogs.
How much did she spend?

_____ X _____ = $_____

_____ X _____ = $_____

_____ X _____ = $_____

Total:
_____ +_____ + _____ = $_____

3, 6 and 9 Magic Review

Fill in tables 3, 6 and 9.

X	1	2	3	4	5	6	7	8	9	10
1										
2										
3										
4										
5										
6										
7										
8										
9										
10										

Name _____

Magic Circus Fun

Help Rudy multiply the following:
Step 1) multiply. Step 2) write the rule for Odds & Evens.

___ x ___ = ___
___ x ___ = EVEN

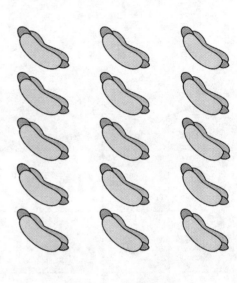

___ x ___ = ___
___ x ___ = ODD

___ x ___ = ___
___ x ___ = ___

___ x ___ = ___
___ x ___ = ___

One More Time with 3, 6 and 9!

Look at the examples and fill in the chart.
Don't forget the 2 steps with 48. ***Good job!***

X	3	Add	6	Add	9	Add
1	3	0+3=	6	0+6=	9	0+9=
2	6	0+6=	12		18	
3	9	0+9=	18		27	
4	12		24		36	
5	15		30		45	
6	18		36		54	
7	21		42		63	
8	24		48		72	
9	27		54		81	
10	30		60		90	

Color the Clown

Solve the problems to color the clown. Choose your own colors for the face and hat.

Color Key

6 - yellow
12 - red
18 - green
24 - blue
36 - orange
40 - purple

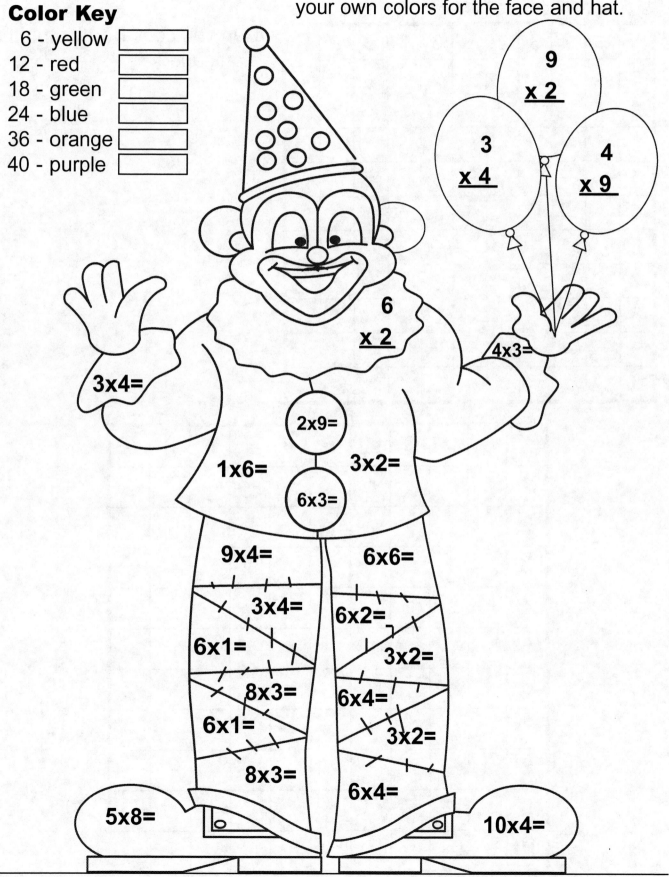

9×2

3×4

4×9

6×2

$4 \times 3 =$

$3 \times 4 =$

$2 \times 9 =$

$1 \times 6 =$

$3 \times 2 =$

$6 \times 3 =$

$9 \times 4 =$

$6 \times 6 =$

$3 \times 4 =$

$6 \times 2 =$

$6 \times 1 =$

$3 \times 2 =$

$8 \times 3 =$

$6 \times 4 =$

$6 \times 1 =$

$3 \times 2 =$

$8 \times 3 =$

$6 \times 4 =$

$5 \times 8 =$

$10 \times 4 =$

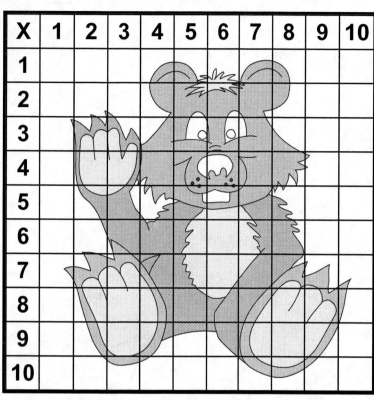

Can you copy Bernice on the blank grid?

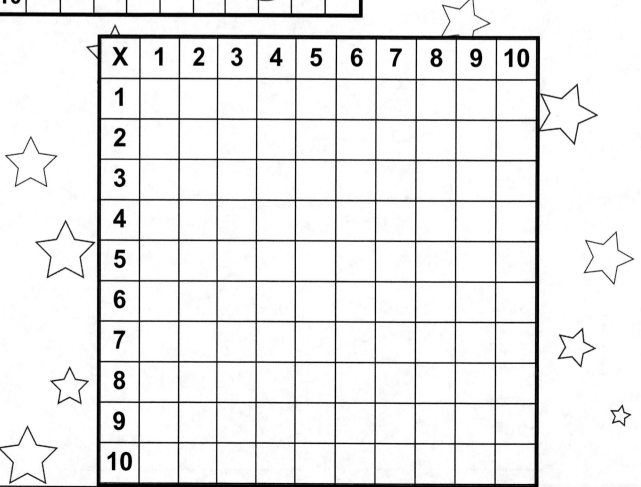

Name _____

Amazing Clue to the 7's

If you know your 3 x table, you know your 7's.
Take the <u>underlined digit</u> in the 3 x table **reversed**
and fill in the 7 x table. **Pretty amazing!.**

X		3 x table Reversed	7
0	10	3<u>0</u>	<u>0</u>
1	9	2<u>7</u>	_
2	8	2<u>4</u>	1_
3	7	2<u>1</u>	2_
4	6	1<u>8</u>	2_
5	5	1<u>5</u>	3_
6	4	1<u>2</u>	4_
7	3	<u>9</u>	4_
8	2	<u>6</u>	5_
9	1	<u>3</u>	6_
10	0	<u>0</u>	7_

Amazing Clue Review

Fill in the blanks.

X		3 x table Reversed	7
0	10	3_0_	_0_
1	9	2_7_	7
2	8	2_	1_
3	7	2_	2_
4	6	1_	2_
5	5	1_	3_
6	4	1_	4_
7	3	_	4_
8	2	_	5_
9	1	_	6_
10	0	_0_	7_

Name _____

What Are the Odds?

Help Rudy group in pairs. Example:

Any ODD 🐒 , ▭ , ◿ , 🥜 left over?
Write a multiplication problem for each.

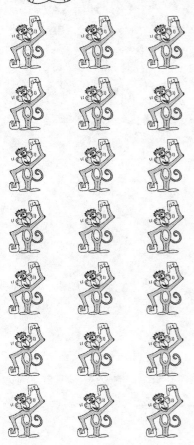

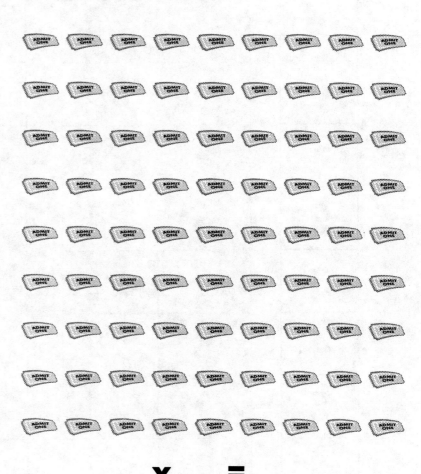

__ **X** __ = __   __ **X** __ = __

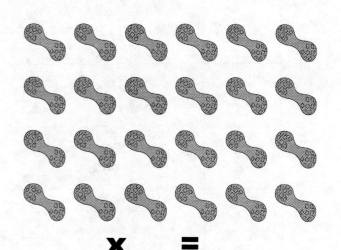

__ **X** __ = __   __ **X** __ = __

7's Challenge!

Fill in the 7 table.

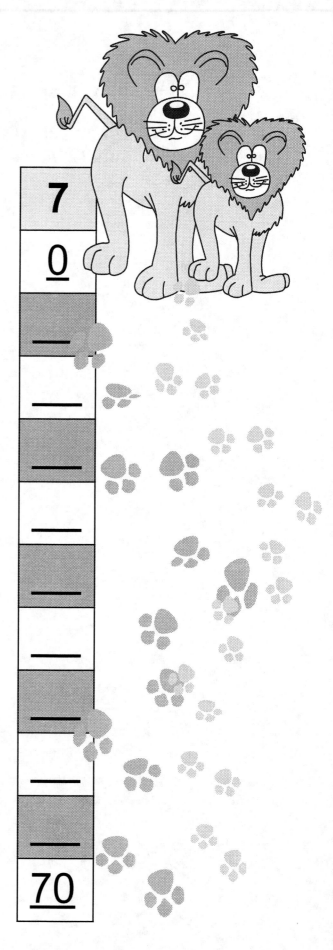

X		3 x table Reversed	7
0	10	3_0_	_0_
1	9	2_7_	___
2	8	2_4_	___
3	7	2_1_	___
4	6	1_8_	___
5	5	1_5_	___
6	4	1_2_	___
7	3	_9_	___
8	2	_6_	___
9	1	_3_	___
10	0	_0_	_70_

Fill in the blanks.

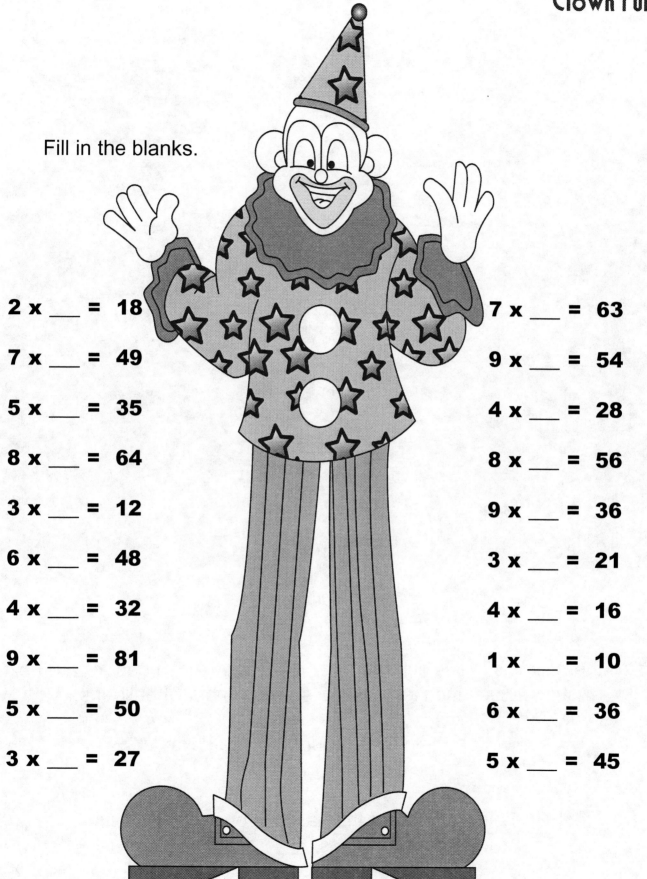

2 x ___ = 18

7 x ___ = 49

5 x ___ = 35

8 x ___ = 64

3 x ___ = 12

6 x ___ = 48

4 x ___ = 32

9 x ___ = 81

5 x ___ = 50

3 x ___ = 27

7 x ___ = 63

9 x ___ = 54

4 x ___ = 28

8 x ___ = 56

9 x ___ = 36

3 x ___ = 21

4 x ___ = 16

1 x ___ = 10

6 x ___ = 36

5 x ___ = 45

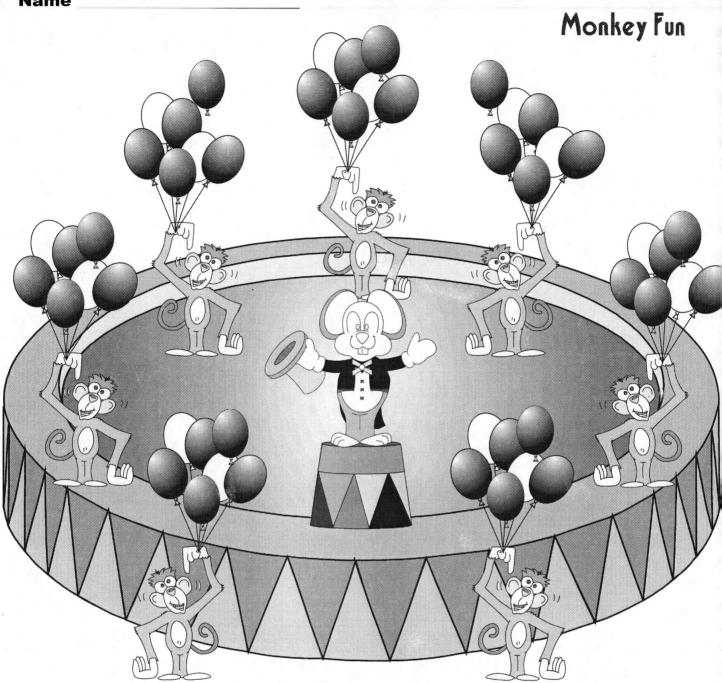

If all the balloons in this act pop, how many will Rudy need for the next
show? Each monkey has the same number of balloons.

Let's help Rudy count the monkeys.
There are _____ monkeys.

Let's help Rudy count the balloons one monkey has.
Each monkey has _____ balloons.

_____ x _____ = _____ balloons

Name _____

Magic Circus Fun

Missing Evens!

Fill in the blanks.

3 x ___ = 24	8 x ___ = 64	6 x ___ = 24
6 x ___ = 12	5 x ___ = 30	7 x ___ = 28
1 x ___ = 10	9 x ___ = 72	5 x ___ = 20
3 x ___ = 18	4 x ___ = 16	3 x ___ = 30
2 x ___ = 16	5 x ___ = 40	5 x ___ = 10
7 x ___ = 14	9 x ___ = 36	9 x ___ = 54
5 x ___ = 50	4 x ___ = 32	2 x ___ = 20
8 x ___ = 48	9 x ___ = 18	6 x ___ = 48
4 x ___ = 24	8 x ___ = 32	7 x ___ = 42
8 x ___ = 16	7 x ___ = 56	4 x ___ = 40
3 x ___ = 12	8 x ___ = 80	6 x ___ = 36
9 x ___ = 90	**Good Job!**	7 x ___ = 70

Magic Circus Fun

Missing Odds!

Fill in the blanks.

7 x ___ = 21	3 x ___ = 15	9 x ___ = 81
5 x ___ = 35	6 x ___ = 30	2 x ___ = 18
6 x ___ = 54	8 x ___ = 72	5 x ___ = 45
4 x ___ = 28	2 x ___ = 10	8 x ___ = 40
3 x ___ = 21	4 x ___ = 20	6 x ___ = 42
2 x ___ = 14	7 x ___ = 49	9 x ___ = 45
8 x ___ = 24	9 x ___ = 27	7 x ___ = 63
6 x ___ = 18	4 x ___ = 36	5 x ___ = 15
3 x ___ = 27	8 x ___ = 56	7 x ___ = 35
4 x ___ = 12	2 x ___ = 6	9 x ___ = 63
5 x ___ = 25	**Good Job!**	10 x ___ = 90

Name _____

Help Bernice complete the pattern
and find her way home to
175 Magic Circus Drive.

7   14   21

70

Bernice

140

175

HONEY

Grid Magic

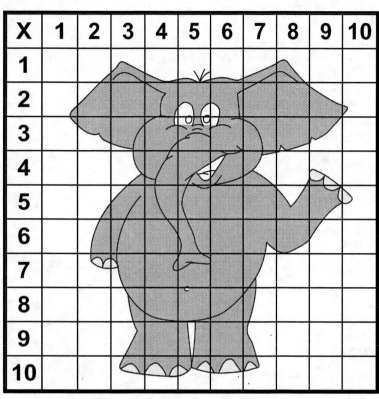

Can you copy Bertha on the blank grid?

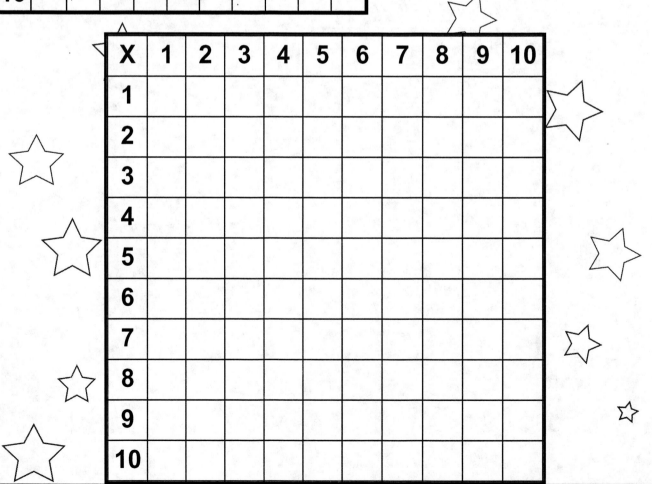

The Lonely Odds
Odd x Odd = Odd

Fill in the squares for Odd x Odd with an **o** for **ODD**.
Notice the **hopscotch** pattern for **ODD** numbers.
How many squares did you fill in?
Out of 100 multiples
_____ were ODD.

X	1	2	3	4	5	6	7	8	9	10
1										
2										
3										
4										
5										
6										
7										
8										
9										
10										

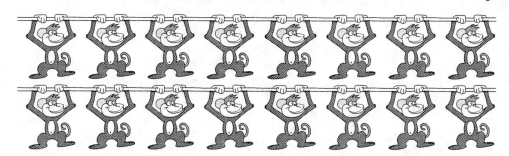

__ x __ = __ s

__ x __ = __ s

__ x __ = __ s

Dots Squared

Squaring a number is multiplying the number times itself.
Notice the square formed by 2 x 2, 3 x 3, 4 x 4 and 5 x 5.
Pretty cool!

X	1	2	3	4	5
1	•	••	•••	••••	•••••
2	⠒	⠒⠒	⠒⠒⠒	⠒⠒⠒⠒	⠒⠒⠒⠒⠒
3	⠇	⠇⠇	⠇⠇⠇	⠇⠇⠇⠇	⠇⠇⠇⠇⠇
4	⠿	⠿⠿	⠿⠿⠿	⠿⠿⠿⠿	⠿⠿⠿⠿⠿
5	⦙	⦙⦙	⦙⦙⦙	⦙⦙⦙⦙	⦙⦙⦙⦙⦙

Fun Squaring Numbers

A number multiplied times itself creates a square on the grid.
Start with the single SQUARE of 1 x 1 and step by step
go down the 100 square grid of 10 x 10.
Notice how the squares get larger and larger.
Outline each additional square a different color.
How many squares did you end up with? ____

X	1	2	3	4	5	6	7	8	9	10
1	1									
2		4								
3			9							
4				16						
5					25					
6						36				
7							49			
8								64		
9									81	
10										100

Name _____

Here's the Answer!
What's the Problem?

Fill in the blanks. If an answer appears twice, give another
possibility using different numbers. Do not multiply by 1.

Example: __3 x 4__ = 12   or   __6 x 2__ = 12

___ x ___ = 40   ___ x ___ = 40   ___ x ___ = 18

___ x ___ = 18   ___ x ___ = 9   ___ x ___ = 15

___ x ___ = 24   ___ x ___ = 24   ___ x ___ = 16

___ x ___ = 16   ___ x ___ = 10   ___ x ___ = 48

___ x ___ = 30   ___ x ___ = 25   ___ x ___ = 36

___ x ___ = 36   ___ x ___ = 64   ___ x ___ = 14

___ x ___ = 63   ___ x ___ = 72   ___ x ___ = 35

___ x ___ = 81   ___ x ___ = 27   ___ x ___ = 42

___ x ___ = 32   ___ x ___ = 60   ___ x ___ = 6

___ x ___ = 54   ___ x ___ = 56   ___ x ___ = 21

___ x ___ = 45   ___ x ___ = 28   ___ x ___ = 50

___ x ___ = 12   ___ x ___ = 12   ___ x ___ = 0

___ x ___ = 20   **Good Job!**   ___ x ___ = 20

Squaring Numbers Review

What is 1 x 1? 2 x 2? 3 x 3? 4 x 4? 5 x 5?
6 x 6? 7 x 7? 8 x 8? 9 x 9? 10 x 10?
Fill in the __.

X	1	2	3	4	5	6	7	8	9	10
1	1									
2		_								
3			_							
4				_						
5					_					
6						_				
7							_			
8								_		
9									_	
10										_

How many clowns in total? _____ x _____ = _____

How many monkeys in total? _____ x _____ = _____

How many lions in total? _____ x _____ = _____

How many giraffes in total? _____ x _____ = _____

Circus Fun

Help Rudy multiply the following.
Underneath, write the Odd/Even rule.

6 x 4   = ____   3 x 3   = ____   8 x ___ = 48

<u>e</u> x <u>e</u>   = EVEN   ___ x ___ = ____   ___ x ___ = ____

2 x ___ = 12   6 x 3   = ____   5 x ___ = 30

___ x ___ = ____   ___ x ___ = ____   ___ x ___ = ____

6 x 7   = ____   3 x 10 = ____   9 x ___ = 54

___ x ___ = ____   ___ x ___ = ____   ___ x ___ = ____

7 x ___ = 63   9 x ___ = 81   3 x ___ = 15

___ x ___ = ____   ___ x ___ = ____   ___ x ___ = ____

9 x ___ = 63   3 x ___ = 21   5 x ___ = 45

___ x ___ = ____   ___ x ___ = ____   ___ x ___ = ____

5 x 7   = ____   4 x ___ = 12   3 x 9   = ____

___ x ___ = ____   ___ x ___ = ____   ___ x ___ = ____

9 x ___ = 72   3 x ___ = 24   9 x 4   = ____

___ x ___ = ____   ___ x ___ = ____   ___ x ___ = ____

Solve the Missing Diagonal

Fill in the missing diagonal.
Remember **Odd x Odd = Odd.**
Even x Even = Even.

X	1	2	3	4	5	6	7	8	9	10
1		2	3	4	5	6	7	8	9	10
2	2		6	8	10	12	14	16	18	20
3	3	6		12	15	18	21	24	27	30
4	4	8	12		20	24	28	32	36	40
5	5	10	15	20		30	35	40	45	50
6	6	12	18	24	30		42	48	54	60
7	7	14	21	28	35	42		56	63	70
8	8	16	24	32	40	48	56		72	80
9	9	18	27	36	45	54	63	72		90
10	10	20	30	40	50	60	70	80	90	

Odd Number Diagonals

Fill in the diagonals.
Notice how numbers repeat on either side.
Wow, it's like magic!

X	1	2	3	4	5	6	7	8	9	10
1	1		3		5					
2		4		8						
3	3		9							
4		8		16						
5	5			25						
6						36				
7							49			
8								64		
9									81	
10										100

Even Number Diagonals

Fill in the diagonals. What did you discover
about diagonal patterns for EVEN numbers?

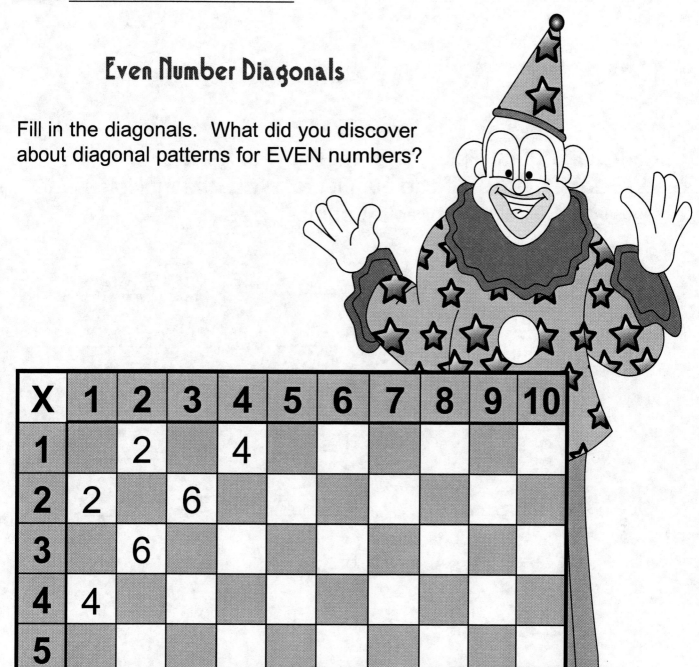

X	1	2	3	4	5	6	7	8	9	10
1		2		4						
2	2		6							
3		6								
4	4									
5										
6										
7										
8										
9										
10										

Odd or Even?

Instead of multiples, fill in with **odd** or **even**.
Secret Clue: if one number is **even**, the multiple is
even. Circle every **even** number first.

☐4☐ x 3 = <u>even</u>	3 x 5 = <u>odd</u>	☐6☐ x ☐2☐ = <u>even</u>
5 x 7 = ____	4 x 8 = ____	3 x 3 = ____
6 x 3 = ____	5 x 8 = ____	9 x 7 = ____
9 x 9 = ____	6 x 9 = ____	7 x 8 = ____
6 x 6 = ____	3 x 9 = ____	2 x 4 = ____
5 x 5 = ____	2 x 6 = ____	8 x 1 = ____
4 x 7 = ____	7 x 5 = ____	2 x 3 = ____
9 x 2 = ____	4 x 4 = ____	5 x 9 = ____
3 x 1 = ____	3 x 8 = ____	7 x 3 = ____
7 x 7 = ____	6 x 8 = ____	8 x 3 = ____
8 x 8 = ____	8 x 7 = ____	9 x 5 = ____
5 x 2 = ____	4 x 5 = ____	7 x 1 = ____

Cool Diagonals!

With a ruler, draw diagonals using a different color for each.
Notice for **EVEN** numbers, the pattern *duplicates* itself.
The diagonal for **4** (which has **4** numbers) is: **4, 6, 6, 4.**

For **ODD** numbers, a number in the **middle** breaks the pattern.
The diagonal for **5** (which has **5** numbers) is: 5, 8, 9, 8, 5.

How many numbers in the diagonals for 3, 6, 7, 8, 9 and 10?
Pretty cool!

X	1	2	3	4	5	6	7	8	9	10
1	1	2	3	4	5	6	7	8	9	10
2	2	4	6	8	10	12	14	16	18	20
3	3	6	9	12	15	18	21	24	27	30
4	4	8	12	16	20	24	28	32	36	40
5	5	10	15	20	25	30	35	40	45	50
6	6	12	18	24	30	36	42	48	54	60
7	7	14	21	28	35	42	49	56	63	70
8	8	16	24	32	40	48	56	64	72	80
9	9	18	27	36	45	54	63	72	81	90
10	10	20	30	40	50	60	70	80	90	100

Odds & Evens

Fill in the blanks.
Underneath complete the rule.

$8 \times \underline{4} = 32$ $7 \times \underline{\ \ } = 21$ $9 \times \underline{\ \ } = 54$

e x <u>e</u> = e   o x __ = o   o x __ = e

$3 \times \underline{\ \ } = 24$ $5 \times \underline{\ \ } = 25$ $2 \times \underline{\ \ } = 18$

o x __ = e   o x __ = o   e x __ = e

$9 \times \underline{\ \ } = 63$ $7 \times \underline{\ \ } = 28$ $4 \times \underline{\ \ } = 20$

o x __ = o   o x __ = e   e x __ = e

$6 \times \underline{\ \ } = 42$ $4 \times \underline{\ \ } = 36$ $5 \times \underline{\ \ } = 45$

e x __ = e   e x __ = e   o x __ = o

$3 \times \underline{\ \ } = 27$ $8 \times \underline{\ \ } = 64$ $9 \times \underline{\ \ } = 81$

o x __ = o   e x __ = e   o x __ = o

Diagonal Flip Flop

Fill in the diagonals.
What did you discover?
Multiplication is super easy!

X	1	2	3	4	5	6	7	8	9	10
1	1	2	3	4						
2	2	4	6							
3	3	6	9							
4	4	8	12	16						
5	5	10	15	20	25					
6	6	12	18	24	30	36				
7	7	14	21	28	35	42	49			
8	8	16	24	32	40	48	56	64		
9	9	18	27	36	45	54	63	72	81	
10	10	20	30	40	50	60	70	80	90	100

Name _____

Grid Magic

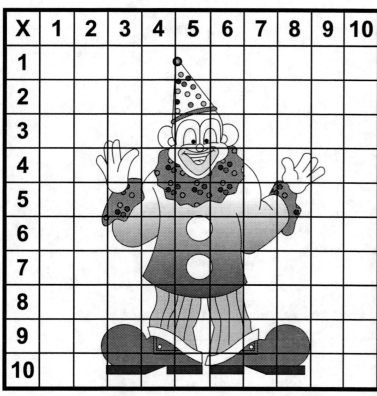

Can you copy Coco on the blank grid?

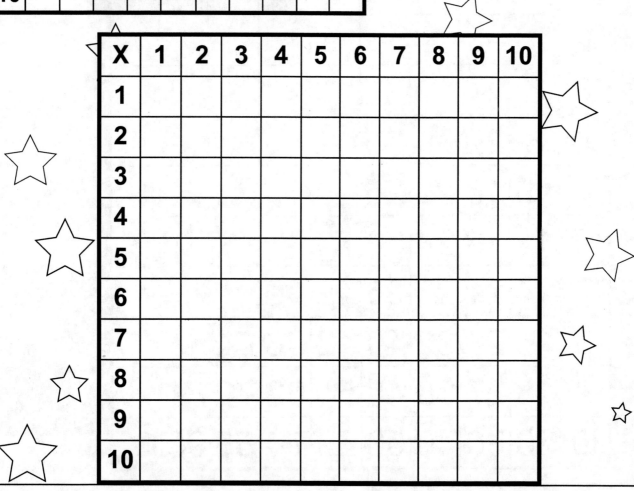

Name _____

Diagonal Flip Flop

Fill in the diagonals.
What did you discover?
Numbers are magic!

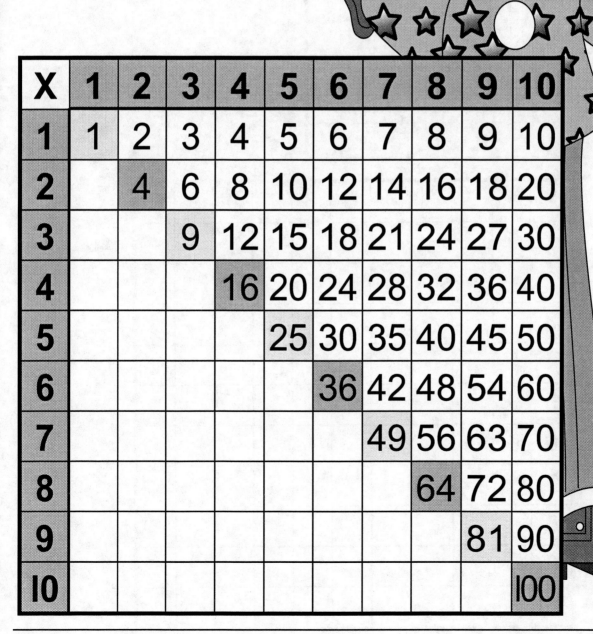

X	1	2	3	4	5	6	7	8	9	10
1	1	2	3	4	5	6	7	8	9	10
2		4	6	8	10	12	14	16	18	20
3			9	12	15	18	21	24	27	30
4				16	20	24	28	32	36	40
5					25	30	35	40	45	50
6						36	42	48	54	60
7							49	56	63	70
8								64	72	80
9									81	90
10										100

Grid Magic

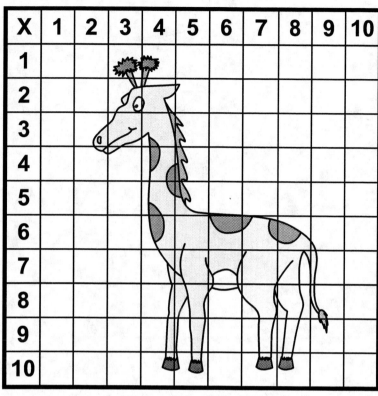

Can you copy Gia on the blank grid?

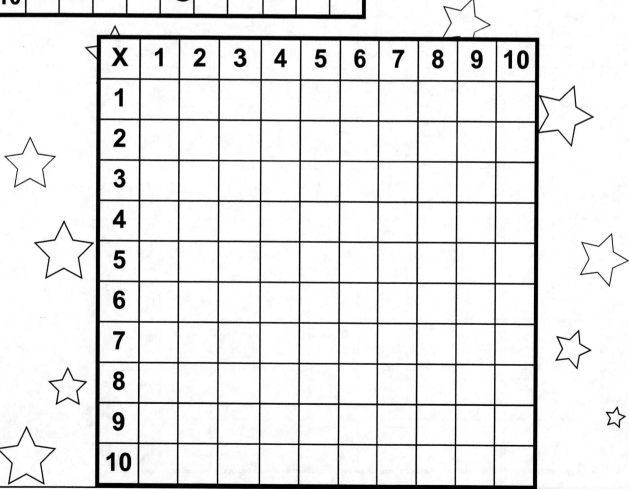

Name _____

Decoding Patterns?
Write the multiplication problem for:

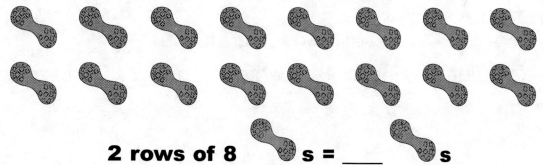

2 rows of 8 **s = ___** **s**

2 x 8 = ___

even x even = ___

___ rows of ___  **s = ___**  **s**

___ x ___ = ___

odd x ___ = ___

___ rows of ___  **s = ___**  **s**

___ x ___ = ___

odd x ___ = ___

You Know the Rules!

Fill in the blanks. Underneath write the rule for Odds and Evens.

2 x ____ = 14   3 x ____ = 21   5 x ____ = 40

_____   _____   _____

9 x ____ = 36   7 x ____ = 42   4 x ____ = 32

_____   _____   _____

3 x ____ = 24   5 x ____ = 20   6 x ____ = 54

_____   _____   _____

8 x ____ = 48   2 x ____ = 12   7 x ____ = 49

_____   _____   _____

6 x ____ = 24   9 x ____ = 72   5 x ____ = 15

_____   _____   _____

7 x ____ = 63   8 x ____ = 56   2 x ____ = 16

_____   _____   _____

Super **X** Diagonals?

Name _____

Fill in the diagonals.
Notice how the multiples in the top and left sides match.
So do the bottom and right sides.
Why is that? *Pretty cool!*

X	1	2	3	4	5	6	7	8	9	10
1		2	3	4	5	6	7	8	9	
2	2		6	8	10	12	14	16		20
3	3	6		12	15	18	21		27	30
4	4	8	12		20	24		32	36	40
5	5	10	15	20			35	40	45	50
6	6	12	18	24			42	48	54	60
7	7	14	21		35	42		56	63	70
8	8	16		32	40	48	56		72	80
9	9		27	36	45	54	63	72		90
10		20	30	40	50	60	70	80	90	

Grid Magic

Can you copy Bip on the blank grid?

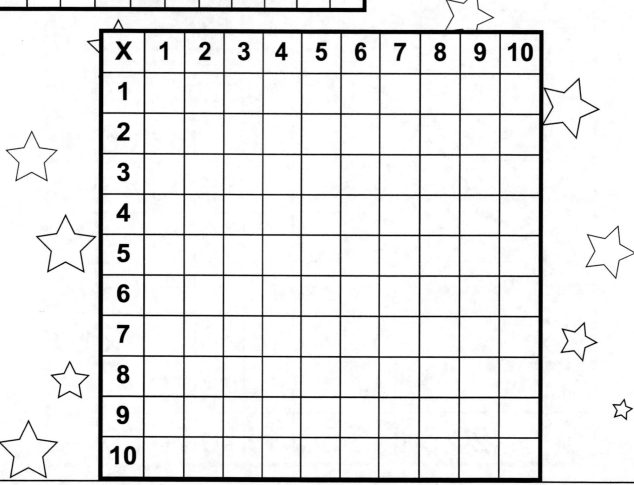

ODDS Diagonal Challenge!

Fill in the white squares. **Secret clue** - to work really fast, fill
in the diagonal 1 - 100 **first** and then the multiples on **either side.**
You'll soon discover a super easy *mirror pattern!*

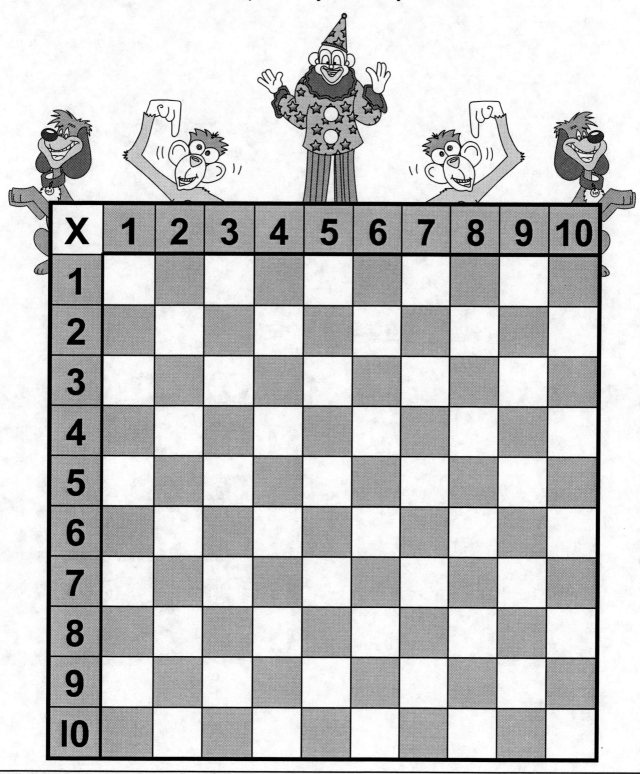

X	1	2	3	4	5	6	7	8	9	10
1										
2										
3										
4										
5										
6										
7										
8										
9										
10										

Name _____

Magic Circus Fun

Help Rudy multiply the following:
Step 1) multiply. Step 2) write the rule for Odds & Evens.

_____ x _____ = _____

ODD x _____ = _____

_____ x _____ = _____   _____ x _____ = _____

_____ x _____ = _____   _____ x _____ = _____

124   TeaCHildMath™

EVENS diagonal Challenge!

Fill in the white squares.

X	1	2	3	4	5	6	7	8	9	10
1										
2										
3										
4										
5										
6										
7										
8										
9										
10										

Let's Review the Odds

Fill in the missing numbers in tables 1, 3, 5, 7 & 9.
Notice odd/even **hopscotch** pattern.

X	1		3		5		7		9
1	__		__		__		__		__
2	__		__		1_		1_		1_
3	__		__		1_		2_		2_
4	__		1_		2_		2_		3_
5	__		1_		2_		3_		4_
6	__		1_		3_		4_		5_
7	__		2_		3_		4_		6_
8	__		2_		4_		5_		7_
9	__		2_		4_		6_		8_
10	1_		3_		5_		7_		9_

Decoding Patterns

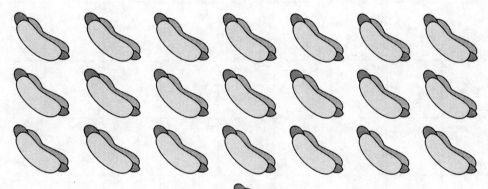

2 rows of 9 🚲s = _____ 🚲s

2 x 9 = ___

even x ___ = ___

___ rows of ___ 🌭s = ___ 🌭 s

___ x ___ = ____
___ x odd = ____

___ rows of ___ 🌂 s = ___ 🌂 s

___ x ___ = ____
___ x ___ = ____

Name _____

Once Again With Odds and Evens

Fill in each square with an **e** for **Even** or an **o** for **Odd**.
Notice the **hopscotch** pattern for **ODD** numbers.
Amazing fact:
Even x Even = EVEN
Even x Odd = EVEN
Odd x Odd = ODD

X	1	2	3	4	5	6	7	8	9	10
1	o	e								
2	e	e								
3										
4										
5										
6										
7										
8										
9										
10										

Shy Numbers?

Circle all the numbers that appear only ONCE on the grid.
How many are there? _____

X	1	2	3	4	5	6	7	8	9	10
1	1	2	3	4	5	6	7	8	9	10
2	2	4	6	8	10	12	14	16	18	20
3	3	6	9	12	15	18	21	24	27	30
4	4	8	12	16	20	24	28	32	36	40
5	5	10	15	20	25	30	35	40	45	50
6	6	12	18	24	30	36	42	48	54	60
7	7	14	21	28	35	42	49	56	63	70
8	8	16	24	32	40	48	56	64	72	80
9	9	18	27	36	45	54	63	72	81	90
10	10	20	30	40	50	60	70	80	90	100

Super Easy Zero!

Help Rudy multiply the following:

4 x 30 = __
4 x 30 = __0

How to solve?
Put the zero on the right.
Multiply **4 x 3**
.

4 x 30 = 12__0
4 x 30 = 120

Put **12** to the left of the zero.
Super easy, isn't it?

4 x 300 = __
4 x 300 = __00

How to solve?
Put the zeroes on the right.
Multiply **4 x 3**.

4 x 300 = 12__00
4 x 300 = 1200

Put **12** to the left of the zeroes.
How easy is that?

Multiply:

3 x 80 = _____

6 x 30 = _____

9 x 70 = _____

5 x 10 = _____

90 x 2 = _____

20 x 8 = _____

50 x 7 = _____

3 x 800 = _____

6 x 300 = _____

9 x 700 = _____

5 x 100 = _____

900 x 2 = _____

200 x 8 = _____

500 x 7 = _____

Circus Tickets

Adults $5

Children $2

Joe's big brother bought 20 children's tickets. How much did he spend?

$2 x 20 = $____

Mrs. Smith bought 30 adult tickets. How much did she spend?

____ x ____ = $____

Coach bought 40 children's tickets and 10 adult tickets. How much did he spend?

40 x ____ = $____
10 x ____ = $____

$____
+ ____
Total: $____

Lisa bought 20 adult tickets and 40 children's tickets. How much did she spend?

___ x ____ = $____
___ x ____ = $____

$____
+ ____
Total: $____

Mr. Villa spent $190 on circus tickets. He spent $40 on children's tickets. How many children's tickets did he buy? How many adult tickets did he buy?

$2 x ____ = $40

Number of children: ____

$190
-$40
Total: $150

$5 x ____ = $150

Number of adults: ____

The school spent $1100 on circus tickets. $500 was spent on adult tickets How many adults went? How many children went?

$5 x ____ = $500

Number of adults: ____

$1100
-$500
Total: $600

$2 x ____ = $600

Number of children: ____

Multiplying Two Digits

First multiply the number on the right. (This is the one's place, next is the ten's.)

```
 1
28     2 x 8 = 16
x2     Write 6 and          ———————→
 6     carry the 1.
```

```
 1
28     2 x 2 = 4
x2     4 + 1 = 5
56     is correct!
```

```
  10        22                    24        18
  x7        x6                    x5        x3
```

```
  15        12                    22        16
  x5        x6                    x5        x3
```

```
  12        25                    45        61
  x9        x4                    x2        x3
```

```
  82        63                    75        42
  x4        x3                    x2        x5
```

Name _____

Circus Snacks

Hot Dogs . . . .$3   Ice Cream $2
Pretzels . . . .$2   Popcorn $3
Cotton Candy . . . .$1   Soda $1

Maria bought 20 pretzels at the circus for her friends.
How much did she spend?

_____ X _____ = $_____

Rico bought his baseball team 30 hot dogs. How much did he spend?

_____ X _____ = $_____

Coach bought 50 bags of popcorn and 40 sodas.
How much did he spend?

_____ X _____ = $_____
_____ X _____ = $_____
Total:
_____ + _____ = $_____

Kim bought 30 ice cream bars and 20 sodas.
How much did she spend?

_____ X _____ = $_____
_____ X _____ = $_____
Total:
_____ + _____ = $_____

Tony and Carla bought the class 60 hotdogs, 50 sodas and 40 ice cream bars. How much did they spend?

_____ X _____ = $_____
_____ X _____ = $_____
_____ X _____ = $_____
Total:
_____ + _____ + _____ = $_____

Julia's mom bought the soccer team 60 sodas, 80 pretzels and 50 hot dogs.
How much did she spend?

_____ X _____ = $_____
_____ X _____ = $_____
_____ X _____ = $_____
Total:
_____ + _____ + _____ = $_____

Name _____

Magic Circus Fun

Help Rudy solve the following:

If there are 9 giraffes, how many must Rudy put in each of the
3 rings so that each ring is the same? _____

If there are 15 monkeys, how many must Rudy put in each of the
3 rings so that each ring is the same? _____

If there are 21 lions, how many must Rudy put in each of the
3 rings so that each ring is the same? _____

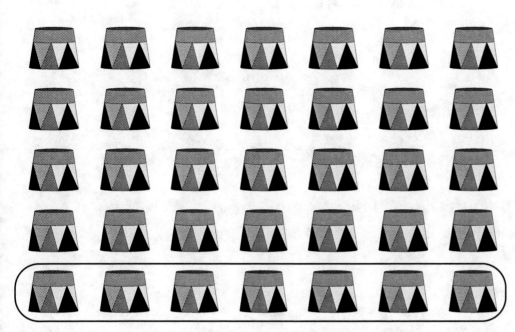

Help Rudy divide 35 equally by 5.

35 ÷ 5 = _____

Is the answer correct? Let's check by multiplying.

5 x _____ = 35

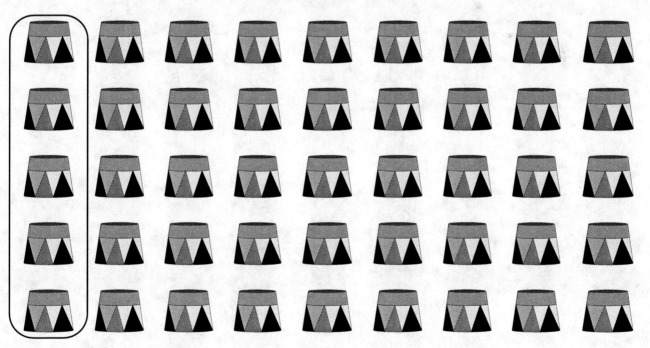

Help Rudy divide 45 equally by 9.

45 ÷ 9 = _____

Is the answer correct? Let's check by multiplying.

9 x _____ = 45

Name _____

Patterns Are Fun!

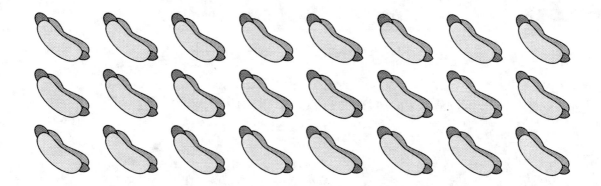

If you divide 20 bicycles in 2 rows,
there will be _____ bicycles in each row.

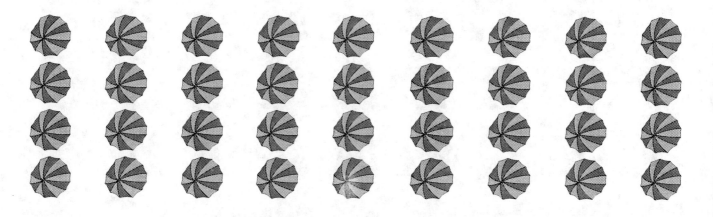

If you divide 24 hot dogs in 3 rows,
there will be _____ hot dogs in each row.

If you divide 36 umbrellas in 4 rows,
there will be _____ umbrellas in each row.

If each circus wagon fits 2 giraffes, how many circus
wagons does Rudy need for 16 giraffes? _____

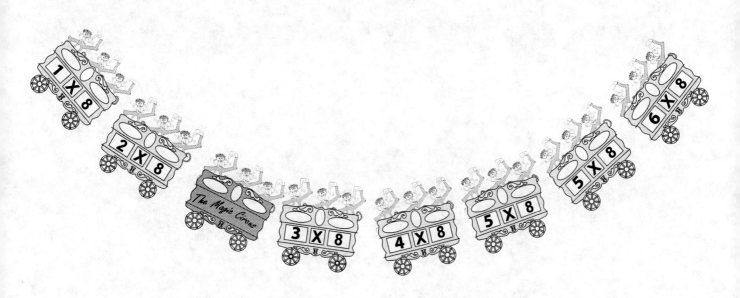

If each circus wagon fits 3 monkeys, how many circus
wagons does Rudy need for 24 monkeys? _____

Magic Circus Acts

Help Rudy divide 15 clowns into three rings
so that the same number is in each ring.

Before

After

Is this correct? If not, draw an arrow
sending the extra clown to the correct ring

15 ÷ 3 = _____

3 x _____ = 15

Magic Circus Acts

Let's help Rudy with the Magic Circus.

6 clowns need to do their act. Only 2 fit in each circus wagon.
How many circus wagons does Rudy need for the clowns?

6 ÷ 2 = _____

10 giraffes need to do their act. Only 2 fit in each circus wagon.
How many circus wagons does Rudy need for the giraffes?

10 ÷ 2 = _____

12 monkeys need to do their act. Only 2 fit in each circus wagon.
How many circus wagons does Rudy need for the monkeys?

12 ÷ 2 = _____

How many circus wagons will Rudy need in total?

_____ + _____ + _____ = _____

Name _____

Patterns Are Fun!

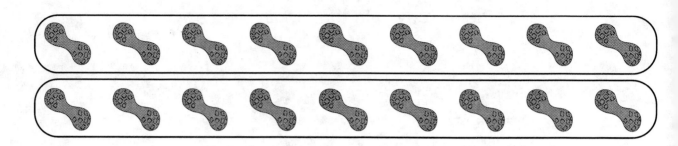

Divide 18 s into 2 groups.

18 ÷ 2 = ____ 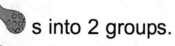 s in each group.

Divide 24 s into 8 groups.

24 ÷ 8 = ____ s in each group.

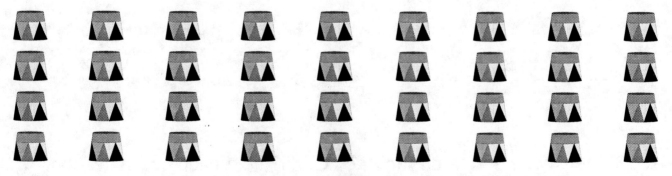

Divide 36 s into 9 groups.

36 ÷ 9 = ____ s in each group.

More Division

Division can be written   20 ÷ 5 = 4

or   5)‾20‾   (with 4 above)

Divide the following:

9)18‾   4)28‾   7)49‾   3)12‾

5)45‾   3)27‾   6)54‾   8)64‾

6)30‾   8)32‾   3)30‾   9)81‾

2)16‾   6)36‾   9)72‾   3)21‾

3)24‾   4)16‾   5)50‾   6)18‾

9)36‾   5)35‾   7)56‾   8)48‾

Let's Do Division!

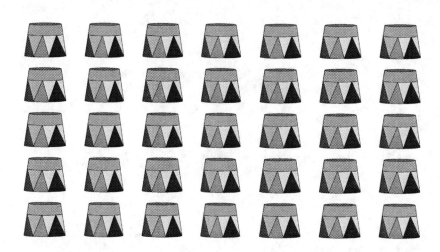

7 x 5 = 35

35 ÷ 5 = 7
or   **35 ÷ 7 = 5**

Turn these multiplication problems into division:

7 x 6 = 42	8 x 9 = 72	4 x 3 = 12
<u>42</u> ÷ <u>6</u> = __7__	___ ÷ ___ = ____	___ ÷ ___ = ____
<u>42</u> ÷ <u>7</u> = __6__	___ ÷ ___ = ____	___ ÷ ___ = ____
6 x 6 = 36	7 x 2 = 14	9 x 5 = 45
___ ÷ ___ = ____	___ ÷ ___ = ____	___ ÷ ___ = ____
___ ÷ ___ = ____	___ ÷ ___ = ____	___ ÷ ___ = ____
4 x 8 = 32	3 x 9 = 27	7 x 7 = 49
___ ÷ ___ = ____	___ ÷ ___ = ____	___ ÷ ___ = ____
___ ÷ ___ = ____	___ ÷ ___ = ____	___ ÷ ___ = ____

Any Remainders?

Example of division <u>without</u> a remainder:

```
    7
5⟌35        5 goes into 35 seven times.
  -35        7 times 5 is 35.  Subtract 35 from 35.
    0        0 left over means NO remainder
```

Example of division <u>with</u> a remainder:

```
    7
5⟌38        5 goes into 38 seven times.
  -35        7 times 5 is 35.  Subtract 35 from 38.
    3        3 is left over.
```

```
   7R3
5⟌38        The answer is written 7R3.
  -35        R means remainder.
    3        Remainder means left over.
             3 was left over.
```

Name _____

Circus Snacks

Hot Dogs . . . .$3   Ice Cream $2
Pizza Slice . . . .$2   Soda $1

Coach bought a large pizza with 24 slices for the team. If each of the 9 players took 2 slices, how many were left over?

9 x 2 = 18 slices   24 − 18 = 6 slices left over

Coach bought a large pizza with 24 slices for the team. If each of the 9 players took the same number of slices, how many slices were left over?

Let's solve by using division:

$$\begin{array}{r} 2 \\ 9\overline{)24} \\ -18 \\ \hline 6 \end{array}$$

9 goes into 24 two times.

9 times 2 is 18. Subtract 18 from 24.

6 is left over.

The answer is written: 2 R6

$$\begin{array}{r} 2\ R6 \\ 9\overline{)24} \\ -\ 18 \\ \hline 6 \end{array}$$

R means remainder
Remainder means left over.
6 slices were left over.

Coach bought the team 20 hot dogs. If each of the 9 players took the same number of hot dogs, how many were left over?

Check your answer. Here are 20 hot dogs.
Circle the hot dogs each of the 9 players got.
Underline the hot dogs left over. These are the remainder.

Name _____

Any Remainders?

Example of division without a remainder:

```
     7
5⌐35        5 goes into 35 seven times.
 -35        7 times 5 is 35.  Subtract 35 from 35.
   0        0 left over means NO remainder
```

Divide the following:

```
   3 R4          8
6⌐22          4⌐32          8⌐74          3⌐17          7⌐30
 - 18          - 32
   4             0
```

```
2⌐19          9⌐45          5⌐48          6⌐38          4⌐18
```

```
7⌐45          3⌐22          6⌐36          5⌐24          9⌐33
```

```
8⌐22          5⌐47          3⌐24          6⌐55          4⌐29
```

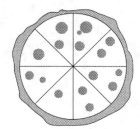 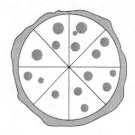 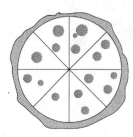

How many slices in each circus pizza? _____

How many slices altogether? ____ x ____ = _____

If coach had 3 slices, how many slices of pizza were left for the team?
(Clue: with a marker cross out 1 slice in each pizza.)

____ - ____ = ____

If the 7 team members shared the remaining slices equally, how many slices did each have?

_____ ÷ ___ = _____

If the pizzas cost $12 each, how much did coach spend on 3 pizzas?

____ x _____ = $ _____

If coach bought 20 sodas at $2 each, how much did he spend on sodas?

____ x ____ = $ _____

If coach spent $19 on circus tickets, how much did he spend at the circus including pizza and sodas?

____ + ____ + ____ = $ _____

If coach handed the cashier a $100 bill, how much change did he get?

_____ - ____ = $_____

Name _____

C-r-a-z-y Scramble

Fill in the grid with the
correct multiple:

X	3	6	9	7	2	8	4	5	1	10
3										
6										
9										
7										
2										
8										
4										
5										
1										
10										

C-r-a-z-y Scramble

Fill in the grid with the correct multiple:

X	10	9	8	7	6	5	4	3	2	1
10										
9										
8										
7										
6										
5										
4										
3										
2										
1										

Name _____

C-r-a-z-y Scramble

Fill in the grid with the
correct multiple:

X	2	5	9	3	10	4	1	6	7	8
7										
4										
5										
1										
10										
2										
8										
3										
6										
9										

C-r-a-z-y Scramble

Create your own!

Multiple Mystery?

Not all the multiples are complete. Fill in the _____.

X	1	2	3	4	5	6	7	8	9	10
1	1	2	3	4	5	6	7	8	9	_0
2	2	4	6	8	_0	_2	_4	_6	_8	20
3	3	6	9	_2	_5	_8	21	24	27	30
4	4	8	_2	_6	20	24	28	32	36	40
5	5	_0	_5	20	25	30	35	40	45	50
6	6	_2	_8	24	30	36	42	48	54	60
7	7	_4	21	28	35	42	49	56	63	70
8	8	_6	24	32	40	48	56	64	72	80
9	9	_8	27	36	45	54	63	72	81	90
10	_0	20	30	40	50	60	70	80	90	100

Name _____

Multiple Mystery?

Not all the multiples are complete.
Fill in the _____.

X	1	2	3	4	5	6	7	8	9	10
1	1	2	3	4	5	6	7	8	9	10
2	2	4	6	8	10	12	14	16	18	_0
3	3	6	9	12	15	18	_1	_4	_7	30
4	4	8	12	16	_0	_4	_8	32	36	40
5	5	10	15	_0	_5	30	35	40	45	50
6	6	12	18	_4	30	36	42	48	54	60
7	7	14	_1	_8	35	42	49	56	63	70
8	8	16	_4	32	40	48	56	64	72	80
9	9	18	_7	36	45	54	63	72	81	90
10	10	_0	30	40	50	60	70	80	90	100

152   TeaCHildMath™

Name _____

Multiple Mystery?

Not all the multiples are complete.
Fill in the _____.

X	1	2	3	4	5	6	7	8	9	10
1	1	2	3	4	5	6	7	8	9	10
2	2	4	6	8	10	12	14	16	18	20
3	3	6	9	12	15	18	21	24	27	_0
4	4	8	12	16	20	24	28	_2	_6	40
5	5	10	15	20	25	_0	_5	40	45	50
6	6	12	18	24	_0	_6	42	48	54	60
7	7	14	21	28	_5	42	49	56	63	70
8	8	16	24	_2	40	48	56	64	72	80
9	9	18	27	_6	45	54	63	72	81	90
10	10	20	_0	40	50	60	70	80	90	100

Name _____

Multiple Mystery?

Not all the multiples are complete.
Fill in the _____.

X	1	2	3	4	5	6	7	8	9	10
1	1	2	3	4	5	6	7	8	9	10
2	2	4	6	8	10	12	14	16	18	20
3	3	6	9	12	15	18	21	24	27	30
4	4	8	12	16	20	24	28	32	36	_0
5	5	10	15	20	25	30	35	_0	_5	50
6	6	12	18	24	30	36	_2	_8	54	60
7	7	14	21	28	35	_2	_9	56	63	70
8	8	16	24	32	_0	_8	56	64	72	80
9	9	18	27	36	_5	54	63	72	81	90
10	10	20	30	_0	50	60	70	80	90	100

TeaCHildMath™

Name _____

Multiple Mystery?

Not all the multiples are complete.
Fill in the _____.

X	1	2	3	4	5	6	7	8	9	10
1	1	2	3	4	5	6	7	8	9	10
2	2	4	6	8	10	12	14	16	18	20
3	3	6	9	12	15	18	21	24	27	30
4	4	8	12	16	20	24	28	32	36	40
5	5	10	15	20	25	30	35	40	45	_0
6	6	12	18	24	30	36	42	48	_4	60
7	7	14	21	28	35	42	49	_6	63	70
8	8	16	24	32	40	48	_6	64	72	80
9	9	18	27	36	45	_4	63	72	81	90
10	10	20	30	40	_0	60	70	80	90	100

Multiple Mystery for 6, 7, 8 and 9!
Not all the multiples are complete.
Fill in the _____.

X	1	2	3	4	5	6	7	8	9	10
1	1	2	3	4	5	6	7	8	9	10
2	2	4	6	8	10	12	14	16	18	20
3	3	6	9	12	15	18	21	24	27	30
4	4	8	12	16	20	24	28	32	36	40
5	5	10	15	20	25	30	35	40	45	50
6	6	12	18	24	30	36	42	48	54	_0
7	7	14	21	28	35	42	49	56	_3	_0
8	8	16	24	32	40	48	56	_4	_2	_0
9	9	18	27	36	45	54	_3	_2	_1	_0
10	10	20	30	40	50	_0	_0	_0	_0	100

Name _____

Multiple Mystery Review

Not all the multiples are complete. Fill in the _____

X	1	2	3	4	5	6	7	8	9	10
1	1	2	3	4	5	6	7	8	9	_0
2	2	4	6	8	_0	_2	_4	_6	_8	_0
3	3	6	9	_2	_5	_8	_1	_4	_7	_0
4	4	8	_2	_6	_0	_4	_8	_2	_6	_0
5	5	_0	_5	_0	_5	_0	_5	_0	_5	_0
6	6	_2	_8	_4	_0	_6	_2	_8	_4	_0
7	7	_4	_1	_8	_5	_2	_9	_6	_3	_0
8	8	_6	_4	_2	_0	_8	_6	_4	_2	_0
9	9	_8	_7	_6	_5	_4	_3	_2	_1	_0
10	_0	_0	_0	_0	_0	_0	_0	_0	_0	_0

TeaCHildMath™ **157**

Grid Magic

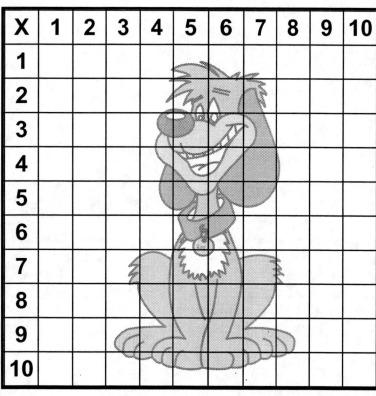

Can you copy Rex on the blank grid?

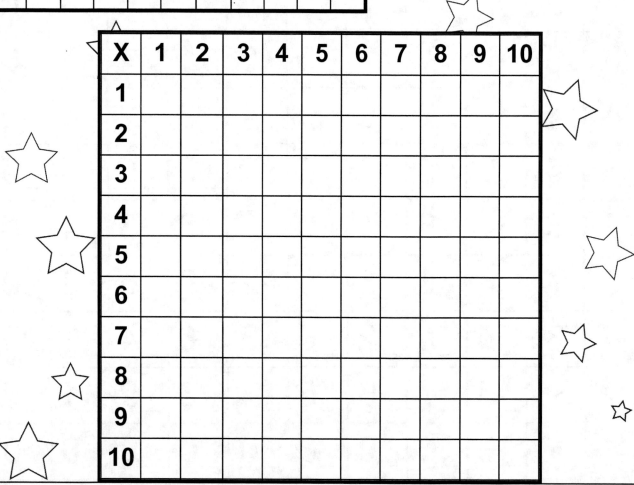

Multiplication *Bingo!*

B	I	N	G	O

Choose 5 Numbers for Each Letter:

B: 1, 2, 3, 4, 5, 6, 7, 8, 9, 10
I: 12, 14, 15, 16, 18, 20, 21, 24
N: 25, 27, 28, 30, 32, 35, 36, 40
G: 42, 45, 48, 49, 50, 54, 56, 60
O: 63, 64, 70, 72, 80, 81, 90, 100

Call out multiplication problem such as 3 x 5 = ?
Student marks answer with an X.

You Go, Even Numbers!

Fill in the grid. Circle **all** the **even** numbers. Did you notice that **ANY** number whether **ODD** or **EVEN** multiplied by an **EVEN** number is **EVEN**?

EVEN x ANY Number = EVEN

X	1	2	3	4	5	6	7	8	9	10
1										
2										
3										
4										
5										
6										
7										
8										
9										
10										

Name _____

Secret Code

2 x table : **2-4-6-8** followed by a **0**.
8 x table : **8-6-4-2** followed by a **0**.
4 x table : **4-8-2-6** followed by a **0**.
6 x table : **6-2-8-4** followed by a **0**.

X	2		8
1	2		8
2	4		16
3	6		24
4	8		32
5	10		40
6	12		48
7	14		56
8	16		64
9	18		72
10	20		80

4		6
4		6
8		12
12		18
16		24
20		30
24		36
28		42
32		48
36		54
40		60

Multiples of Odds and Evens
Amazing Basket Weave Pattern

X	1	2	3	4	5	6	7	8	9	10
1	1	2	3	4	5	6	7	8	9	10
2	2	4	6	8	10	12	14	16	18	20
3	3	6	9	12	15	18	21	24	27	30
4	4	8	12	16	20	24	28	32	36	40
5	5	10	15	20	25	30	35	40	45	50
6	6	12	18	24	30	36	42	48	54	60
7	7	14	21	28	35	42	49	56	63	70
8	8	16	24	32	40	48	56	64	72	80
9	9	18	27	36	45	54	63	72	81	90
10	10	20	30	40	50	60	70	80	90	100

Multiplication Template

X	1	2	3	4	5	6	7	8	9	10
1										
2										
3										
4										
5										
6										
7										
8										
9										
10										

Rudy's Magic Grid

To solve a multiplication problem for numbers 1-10, find one of the numbers in the top row and the other in the column on the far left. Now run your fingers down and accross from these numbers.

Your fingers will meet on the correct answer!

Try it with 6 x 4 =? Did your fingers meet at 24?
Wow, it's like magic!

X	1	2	3	4	5	6	7	8	9	10
1	1	2	3	4	5	6	7	8	9	10
2	2	4	6	8	10	12	14	16	18	20
3	3	6	9	12	15	18	21	24	27	30
4	4	8	12	16	20	24	28	32	36	40
5	5	10	15	20	25	30	35	40	45	50
6	6	12	18	24	30	36	42	48	54	60
7	7	14	21	28	35	42	49	56	63	70
8	8	16	24	32	40	48	56	64	72	80
9	9	18	27	36	45	54	63	72	81	90
10	10	20	30	40	50	60	70	80	90	100

X	1	2	3	4	5	6	7	8	9	10
1	1	2	3	4	5	6	7	8	9	10
2	2	4	6	8	10	12	14	16	18	20
3	3	6	9	12	15	18	21	24	27	30
4	4	8	12	16	20	24	28	32	36	40
5	5	10	15	20	25	30	35	40	45	50
6	6	12	18	24	30	36	42	48	54	60
7	7	14	21	28	35	42	49	56	63	70
8	8	16	24	32	40	48	56	64	72	80
9	9	18	27	36	45	54	63	72	81	90
10	10	20	30	40	50	60	70	80	90	100

Magic Circus Good-by!

Thanks to you,

everyone enjoyed the Magic Circus!

You learned the multiplication tables

and got everything in order.

Monkeys swung on the trapeze.

Lions roared in threes.

Giraffes pranced.

Elephants danced.

Bears tumbled.

Clowns juggled.

The circus was a great success!

Now monkeys, lions, giraffes, elephants, bears

and clowns must board the circus train.

It's time to teach another child.

All of us at the Magic Circus

hope you enjoyed learning

the Multiplication Tables!

Learning is fun!

Pass it on.

A big Magic Circus hooray for you!

Magic Circus Diploma

has mastered
the Multiplication Tables

Date

Signature

PARENT/TEACHER SURVEY

We at the Magic Circus appreciate hearing from parents and teachers

Please comment on your experience with our workbook in teaching your child or classroom the multilication tables. Your input will help us enrich the learning experience of all children.

Log on to **www.TeaCHildMath.com** to share your comments and fill out our questionnaire.

Thank you so much!

Spanish Edition available.